T0319067

Cambridge Elements ≡

Elements in Digital Literary Studies
edited by
Katherine Bode
Australian National University
Adam Hammond
University of Toronto
Gabriel Hankins
Clemson University

LITERARY GEOGRAPHIES IN BALZAC AND PROUST

Melanie Conroy
University of Memphis

CAMBRIDGE
UNIVERSITY PRESS

University Printing House, Cambridge CB2 8BS, United Kingdom

One Liberty Plaza, 20th Floor, New York, NY 10006, USA

477 Williamstown Road, Port Melbourne, VIC 3207, Australia

314–321, 3rd Floor, Plot 3, Splendor Forum, Jasola District Centre,
New Delhi – 110025, India

103 Penang Road, #05–06/07, Visioncrest Commercial, Singapore 238467

Cambridge University Press is part of the University of Cambridge.

It furthers the University's mission by disseminating knowledge in the pursuit of education, learning, and research at the highest international levels of excellence.

www.cambridge.org
Information on this title: www.cambridge.org/9781108994910
DOI: 10.1017/9781108992923

© Melanie Conroy 2021

First published 2021

A catalogue record for this publication is available from the British Library.

ISBN 978-1-108-99491-0 Paperback
ISSN 2633-4399 (online)
ISSN 2633-4380 (print)

Literary Geographies in Balzac and Proust

Elements in Digital Literary Studies

DOI: 10.1017/9781108992923
First published online: November 2021

Melanie Conroy
University of Memphis

Author for correspondence: Melanie Conroy, mrconroy@memphis.edu

Abstract: Literary geography is one of the core aspects of the study of the novel, in both its realist and post-realist incarnations. Literary geography is not just about connecting place-names to locations on the map; literary geographers also explore how spaces interact in fictional worlds and the imaginary of physical space as seen through the lens of characters' perceptions. The tools of literary cartography and geographical analysis can be particularly useful in seeing how places relate to one another and how characters are associated with specific places. This Element explores the literary geographies of Balzac and Proust as exemplary of realist and post-realist traditions of place-making in novelistic spaces. The central concern of this Element is how literary cartography, or the mapping of place-names, can contribute to our understanding of place-making in the novel.

This Element also has a video abstract: www.cambridge.org/conroy

Keywords: literary geography, literary cartography, Balzac, Proust, mapping

ISBNs: 9781108994910 (PB), 9781108992923 (OC)
ISSNs: 2633-4399 (online), 2633-4380 (print)

Contents

1 Introduction: Literary Maps

1.1 What Is Literary Geography?

Literary geography is, first of all, an exploration of place and how place marks literary narratives; as a field, it sits at the intersection of literary studies and human geography (Alexander, 2015). There is more than one way to do literary geography, since literary geography is, as Barbara Piatti has argued, "a topic" rather than a "practice" or a "method" (Piatti et al., 2009; Piatti, 2008). Since setting and spatial relations are core elements of fiction, they have been explored from Marxist, Deleuzian, feminist, psychoanalytic, and other critical approaches that do not necessarily seek to link literary place-names to geographical coordinates. In recent years, Francophone literary geography has opened a conversation between physical geography and literature that has often had a social-scientific bent (Brousseau and Cambron, 2003). Others have made a philosophical turn in the form of *la géocritique*, a critical phenomenological approach to cultural geography that has much in common with postcolonial studies and Deleuzian philosophy (Westphal, 2011), or they have combined *la géocritique* with *la géopoétique*, the analysis of rhetorical structures linked to geography (Collot, 2014). As a topic, literary geography can be approached by way of a number of distinct methods, such as thematic discussion, philological analysis of place-names, or theoretical analysis of "fictional worlds." Indeed, "setting" is such a flexible and ubiquitous concept in literary studies that it can be hard for critics to arrive at one definition. Further, literary geographers can intervene at various levels, exploring themes of place and place-making within fiction at the level of the region, city, or neighborhood.

Literary cartography is a set of practices for mapping and making legible spatial relations within a literary world. In comparison to the concepts of geography or setting, literary cartography has been far more sporadically practiced. Literary maps have, nevertheless, appeared in a variety of literary periods, genres, and schools of literary criticism. Mapping has sometimes been dismissed as positivistic and has played a comparatively minor role in literary criticism despite its long-standing role in book history (Moretti, 1999, pp. 3–6). From maps in medieval manuscripts to map illustrations of the late medieval or early modern texts like Thomas More's *Utopia* and Dante Alighieri's *Divine Comedy*, maps have often served as supports or supplements to texts, both fictional and nonfictional. Works of literary criticism have less often integrated literary cartography than literature itself has done. One of the most audacious and voluminous projects in literary cartography is Malcolm Bradbury's *Atlas of Literature*, a collective work that put forward more than one hundred examples of literary cartography, primarily of realist and modernist works, many in the

English language, starting with Dante and Geoffrey Chaucer and moving through the twentieth century. James Joyce's Dublin, William Faulkner's American South, and Honoré de Balzac and Stendhal's France all feature in Bradbury's edited collection of short essays with illustrated maps of the literary geographies discussed. While the material remains rather general, the *Atlas of Literature* demonstrates the foundational truth for literary geography that, as Bradbury observes in the introduction, a "very large part of our writing is a story of its roots in a place: a landscape, region, village, city, nation or continent" (Bradbury, 1996, n.p.). Bradbury and his coauthors likewise draw attention to geographical patterns within and between literary traditions. The book's designers conceived of a simple method for overlaying toponyms, or place-names, on maps that corresponded roughly to maps that were contemporaneous with the setting of the fiction or the sociohistorical context in which the author lived, many of which are historical maps. My own practice of literary cartography, including the style of the maps in this Element, owes a great deal to the *Atlas of Literature* and other pre-Internet literary geographical projects.

Digital humanities projects that map literary locations and spaces have multiplied in recent years. To name but a few projects focusing on European geography, Barbara Piatti has created *A Literary Atlas of Europe* [*Ein literarischer Atlas Europas*], an atlas of European literary cartography that focuses on Central and Eastern Europe. One of the most attention-grabbing digital humanities studies of place in the European novel was Franco Moretti's *Atlas of the European Novel, 1800–1900*, in which he looked at the geographical distribution of characters and settings, as well as the geography of book circulation, in mostly realist European fiction (Moretti, 1999). From the marriage market in Austen's novels to friend/enemy relations in Balzac, this founding work in literary cartography revealed how mapping social relations among characters could expose the geographical patterns in social relations and hierarchies. In France, there is the Programme de recherche "Vers une géographie littéraire," of the working group l'UMR 7172 THALIM (Théorie et histoire des arts et des littératures de la modernité), a collaboration between the CNRS, the Université Sorbonne nouvelle–Paris 3, and the École Normale Supérieure. At the University of Lancaster, the group "Spatial Humanities: Texts, GIS and Places" has explored mostly British literary geography, especially the Lake District during the Romantic era (Cooper, Donaldson, and Murrieta Flores, 2016).

What, then, are the usual practices of literary cartography? Many digital literary cartographers do find geographical locations that correspond roughly with modern latitudes and longitudes, often mediated by a historical gazetteer or a historical map. Of course, literary maps are culturally determined and do not always correspond exactly to the political and geographical distinctions made by historians and geographers, much less to contemporary divisions of land and peoples. Most literary cartography relies on the modern system of latitudes and longitudes to map the fictional worlds of novels and other fictional works but does not take the cultural and political divisions of the world at face value. Mapping fictional settings requires making base assumptions about how language relates to place; for example, we must decide where the Paris of a particular text is located and how tightly or expansively its geographical boundaries should be drawn. The boundaries of a literary setting may be fragmentary or partial; they may also correspond to a part of a city or other place that is far from the coordinates that designate that place in databases like GeoHack. In my experience, the process of locating a reference on the globe and delimiting its boundaries is not so much a positivistic procedure as an attempt to translate semantics into coordinates in a way that retains as much literary meaning as possible; this process has made me more aware of the vagaries of literary geography. Georeferencing may sound like a simple enough task, but what is meant by "Paris" is surprisingly unstable, varying over time, changing from text to text and even within the same text, fluctuating with the shifting viewpoints of characters. For these reasons, connecting language to a geographical system – in most digital humanities projects, the global information system (GIS) – is not a neutral or unproblematic process (Hill, 2009).

Then there is the question of what we mean by the globe or the global. French studies has borne witness to the many fundamental debates about how the global is cast in literature and literary studies. The edited volume *French Global: A New Approach to Literary History* brought many diverse approaches together in a comparative framework that I have sought to adopt in my own work (McDonald and Suleiman, 2010). But we can do more to pay attention to what is occluded in the articulation of the global. The idea of the global often encodes ideas of center and periphery that perpetuate colonial and postcolonial inequalities. Cities have attracted much attention, with significant projects in literary geography for many European cities; rural areas much less so. Much of the work in European literary geography has focused on themes of travel, exchange, exploitation, and colonialism that are linked to European colonialism rather than the concerns of non-European geographies and peoples. And the global has often been coextensive with human geography to the exclusion of natural environments and nonhuman animals. Notable recent work that is recasting the study of European geographies within a more egalitarian global perspective includes the vast literature on colonial and postcolonial relations; relations with the Pacific, the Caribbean, and the Americas (Lionnet, 1993; Lionnet, 1992); the emergence of digital trans-Atlantic and Atlantic Black studies (Risam and Josephs, 2021); literary geographies of the sea and Island nations in their relation to Europe (Prasad, 2003); and Indigenous literary geographies, all of which play an ever larger role in European literary studies. These are but a few literary critics, topics, and fields that are expanding the connections between European spaces and other geographies without prioritizing European perspectives. By taking on the theme of the global, European literary geography has opened up diverse perspectives, as well as painful stories of exploitation from the perspective of non-European peoples, and literary geographers have discovered previously ignored connections between far-flung locations and peoples as they are reflected in literary works.

1.2 Tools for Digital Literary Cartography

Literary cartography is more accessible than it has been in the past, in large part because of the great number of advanced technologies – from GPS to ArcGIS to Google Maps – that make mapping geographical locations more manageable for non-cartographers and nonexperts. The process of creating a literary map can be at least partially automated at several stages. The first stage is to generate a list of toponyms through the identification and tagging of tokens in a text, which can be extracted automatically (Moncla, Gaio, Joliveau, and Lay, 2017). The second step is to associate these toponyms with modern geographical terms via a gazetteer, which can also be done automatically but often involves manual associations when older place-names lack modern equivalents. This process can be trivial, as I have found it to be at the regional and national levels. It can also be quite tricky, as I have found it to be with streets and smaller buildings located in Paris, a city that has been transformed since the 1830s by the creation of boulevards and wider streets, notably in the 1853–1870 renovation known as Haussmannization; older Parisian streets often bisect modern ones or extend over only a small part of a modern boulevard. Once the toponyms have been extracted, the list of modern place-names can then be geolocated with a geocoder. With a precise list of modern places, this step can be completed mostly automatically, although some homonyms, such as Paris, Texas, may cause trouble. Finally, a list of latitude and longitude coordinates can be placed on a map with visualization software like Google Maps or ArcGIS (Solina and Ravnik, 2010). While these digital tools have equivalents among traditional cartographical tools, automating some of these processes makes literary cartography a far more accessible practice than the painstaking work of georeferencing without digital aids.

Just as automated technologies can help with the extraction of place-names and the construction of maps, the traditional book infrastructures of concordances, indexes, and paper maps can serve as models for digital literary geography projects. The multimedia revolution associated with the development of the Internet and mobile phones has made paratexts and interpretative guides available to more readers and to computer-aided searching. The two corpuses studied here, Honoré de Balzac's *The Human Comedy* [*La Comédie humaine*] and Marcel Proust's *In Search of Lost Time* [*À la recherche du temps perdu*], have been extensively studied for generations from a geographical perspective, as well as for the socioeconomically and psychologically complex fictional worlds they create. Both Balzac's and Proust's toponyms and other place references have been extensively catalogued and analyzed by literary critics. Indeed, Balzac's Paris and Proust's Normandy are often evoked in projects such as Bradbury's *Atlas* and Moretti's *Atlas* because they evoke two seemingly rival models: (1) Balzac's detailed realist model of Paris as a sociologically and economically complex geographical society, and (2) Proust's lightly painted impressionist depictions of Normandy and north-central France. While these two literary geographies are distinct in terms of how much they rely on historical places, I am more interested in how these places relate to global geography than the differences between their French geographies. In their representation of non-French places, these realist and post-realist fictions share a common commitment to historicity and referentiality; indeed, the break from realism to post-realism was never as absolute as has been claimed, nor was realism so thoroughly overthrown as has been argued (Prendergast, 1986). This is as true of geographic representation as of other aspects of literature.

Maps are not the only digital tools that help with the study of literary geographies. In many ways, information visualization has taken the role of indexes and lists of places as the primary medium for the communication of the details of literary geography (Dear, Ketchum, Luria, and Richardson, 2011). Still, these visualizations often build on earlier models for creating and interpreting diagrams (Bender and Merriman, 2010). Even the earliest examples of literary geography often include legends, notes, and other non-cartographical elements. Tools for the visualization of multivariate data sets like R, Tableau, and Palladio let users pair maps with charts and graphs that display non-geographical aspects of multivariate data and data analytics. Visualizations, graphs, and charts can be included with the works themselves or presented in lieu of maps. Digital technology and the Internet have only multiplied the complexity of representations of literary geography, expanding our ability to present interactive visualizations that include maps that can be filtered, that link to images or text, or that display analytics related to parts of maps.

1.3 Characters, Places, and Time

Central to my argument in this Element is the distinction between experienced places and referenced places. Rather than thinking about literary places as either "real" or "fictional," it is productive to see the toponyms used as "historical" if they also occur in historical documents or "nonhistorical" if they do not. Similarly, it is worthwhile to track whether places fit into the narrower category of "experienced" – that is, visited and inhabited by the characters – or the larger, comprehensive category of "referenced" – that is, mentioned, inhabited, or imagined by the narrator or by the characters. Further, even in vast literary geographies, some places are of greater weight and others are merely mentioned in passing. Some places are of greater psychological importance to the characters and some are less noteworthy. In this Element, I review various methods for counting, weighting, and analyzing place references in ways that take account of the literary significance of these references, a process that is not without complications (Bushell, 2016). Literary geography can make use of these quantitative aspects of texts, such as the number of times a geographical term is mentioned in a text. It can also explore the connection of characters and their psychological states, emotions, and the language they use to places within the fictional world; these emotions can be teased out using tools like topic modeling and mapping (Heuser, Algee-Hewitt, and Lockhart, 2016). In realist novels, most of these places may be equivalent to historical places on official maps. However, even in exceptionally geographically realistic texts, literary toponyms can be fluid and their meanings subjective; literary maps, even in realist texts, often function as symbolic maps rather than literal ones (Bray, 2013). There are, moreover, significant differences between literary toponyms and other toponyms, most notably poetic resonances and intertextual references to other literary works. The quantitative study of toponyms is, therefore, a starting point rather than an end point in the interpretation of literary texts.

I have chosen the corpora of Balzac and Proust as case studies because these novelists refer to a similar range of places, some of which are fictional and some of which correspond to historical places. Both Balzac and Proust locate their stories primarily in Paris and a few other provincial French cities and towns while referencing places throughout Europe and, indeed, the world. While Proust's two primary provincial settings, Combray and Balbec, are fictional and Balzac's provincial towns almost all carry the names of historical places, there is a similar imaginative reworking of limited data that applies to places further from Paris regardless of whether the toponyms used correspond to historical places. Due to the salience of Paris and the provinces in both series, the concreteness of international references in both corpora has been less frequently noted. Although the experience of reading Balzac's *The Human*

Comedy and Proust's *In Search of Lost Time* is not necessarily similar, we shall see that they rely on a similar set of tricks and architectural techniques to build a geographical structure for their characters to inhabit; further, that structure departs from the historical world in consistent ways. There is no doubt that Balzac's place references are more numerous across the entirety of *The Human Comedy*, being a much longer text composed of many more books. The proportion of place references by region remains similar, however. Moreover, the level of abstraction in these geographies is more or less coextensive with the fictional world and the experience (both direct and indirect) of the characters who are, for the most part, more familiar with the names of minor streets in Paris than the names of major cities in Africa or the Americas.

Like other computational fields, the digital study of textual and literary geography can fail to take into account nonquantitative elements that are important to the interpretation of the texts studied. Taking a purely "bag of words" approach and counting the occurrences of words or types of words risks missing out on some of the constituent parts of the novel as a genre – notably, textual order and the relation of toponyms to characters and plot. Similarly, looking only at the textual order of geographical references, divorced from the chronological sequence, risks ignoring narrative elements like flashbacks, the interweaving of different timelines, and the pacing of the revelation of the plot (Hones, 2008). This Element looks at the quantitative aspects of geography, how places can be mapped to modern longitudes and latitudes, and how those data can be visualized to make them available to readers, while considering what is not captured in the data. Taking Balzac and Proust as exemplary of novelistic geographies, I present strategies for visualizing literary geographies with large numbers of place references. I draw upon the data of the Mapping Balzac project, a database of all place references in *The Human Comedy* that I have constructed, alongside a data set of the more limited number of place references in Proust.[1] The methods for classifying, visualizing, and analyzing these place references can serve as a model for analyzing other literary texts, most obviously novels, but also fiction or nonfiction that builds up a complex geographical world that is at least partially coextensive with the globe.

2 Balzac's Map of the World

2.1 A Model of Realist Geography

The Human Comedy, a series of more than eighty texts, including novels, essays, and short stories, has been studied as a model of literary geography, mostly for its

---

[1] All of the figures and data for this Element can be downloaded from http://doi.org/10.6084/m9 .figshare.14925177.v1.

detailed maps of Paris and the interconnected industrialized French nation that was coming into being with the era of the railway (Schivelbusch, 1986). Balzac's geography is strongly identified with Paris – and, to a lesser extent, with the French provinces, including his native Touraine, the Loire Valley, and the areas surrounding Paris. Balzac's use of non-French place references – what I am calling Balzac's "map of the world" – has been studied more often from a thematic perspective than cartographically. Although Balzac is one of the great global authors based on the circulation and influence of his works, the predominance of Paris within his fictional world has made references to foreign places less notable. In this section, I look at Balzac's world geography, including Paris and France, but emphasize places outside of France. Using digital mapping, I model the socio-spatial network of one of the first great novelistic series to reveal its truly global footprint. Through the movements of its characters, especially financiers, merchants, and soldiers, *The Human Comedy* traces the growth and decline of the First French Empire and gestures toward some of the military and commercial conflicts to come. The primary settings of *The Human Comedy* are overwhelmingly Parisian or provincial, with the majority in the Hexagon or metropolitan France. It has, however, gone almost unrecognized that *The Human Comedy* refers to places throughout the known world of Balzac's time. While Paris is fundamental to an understanding of the novels, the diversity of referenced places is remarkable for a series of novels that takes place primarily between 1820 and 1840. Only Antarctica, observed for the first time in 1820 and officially discovered in the 1840s, does not figure among the continents referenced.

I take Balzac's geography as a model of realist geography – that is, a fictional world in which most locations correspond roughly to historical locations with the same names and other shared characteristics such as country, language, population, topography, or landmarks.[2] Of course, no fictional world is entirely coextensive with the historical world to which it alludes. Balzac's geography is no exception, with many inventions, errors, and fictional locations not intended to be taken for real places. Yet his fictional world beyond France is predominantly generated in reference to maps and atlases – unsurprising, since he only briefly left France shortly before his death. His interest in foreign countries was cultivated by his father; as a young man, Balzac was very confident in his comprehension of foreign cultures, no doubt overconfident in his knowledge of places like China (Robb, 1995, p. 38). An author can have many reasons for hewing to a realist geography in creating a fictional world, including a sociological or anthropological interest in people or an interest in physical

---

[2] The recent volume *Balzac géographe: territoires* brings together various recent approaches to Balzac's geography (Dufour, Mozet, and Andréoli, 2004).

geography. In Balzac's case, he saw himself as a kind of scientist or naturalist studying various "types" or "species" of the human population, their behaviors, mentalities, and interactions, much as a zoologist would study animal species in their natural habitats. For Balzac, the depictions of faraway locations and peoples in the works of authors like James Fenimore Cooper or Walter Scott were a model for his studies of Parisians and provincials, inverting the usual relation between sociology and anthropology by making the faraway the model for what is known. For Balzac, faraway places are more easily understood scientifically and without bias and descriptions of familiar locations are likely to be less objective. This belief in the systematicity of human behavior leads Balzac to pepper the narration of his fiction, even fictions entirely set in Paris, with references to faraway places and people, often in analogies to the main characters and principal settings of his fiction. The complex network of analogies, together with references to the backstories of minor characters, accounts for many references to far-flung places in Balzac's work.

What complicates this analysis is that Balzac's *The Human Comedy* is not one novel but a series of novels, short stories, and other texts, some of which were finished after the author's death. Some of these texts are humorous; others are quasi-academic essays. Some are hundreds of pages long; others are very brief and tightly plotted. Still, the fictional world and geography obey an overall logic, however haphazardly conceived by the author as he wrote the series. We cannot, therefore, treat Balzac's geography as scientific, as he saw it, nor as disinterested, in the sense of establishing a reliable geographical system of the world as it existed in early nineteenth-century France.[3] Balzac's geography, like the atlases he based it on, is a projection of French power structures. We can make note of the echoes of historical power in Balzac's geography, but we must also be aware of the gaps, the places that do not appear in Balzac or that appear much less than one might expect based on their geographical importance, population, or prominence in the French culture of the era. Even without a comparison to historical geographical knowledge, the many settings, plotlines, and character perspectives of *The Human Comedy* complicate the attribution of any set of ideas or attitudes to Balzac or the series as a whole. The complexity of *The Human Comedy* as a text is a reminder of why a purely quantitative approach is rarely sufficient for literary geography. While there are major quantitative differences in the weighting of various places and their significance in different texts and storylines, the way geographical references

---

[3] Far from being apolitical, cartography and geography were fundamental to the emergence of European states and territories as the major powers used territorial maps as "instruments of rule" in a way that was distinct from cartography in the medieval period or even the early sixteenth century (Biggs, 1999).

appear in a text and how they relate to voice, narration, and characters is equally fundamental to literary analysis.

2.2 A Global Novel

When taken in its entirety, the global geography laid out in the various texts of *The Human Comedy* is vast, despite its disproportionate focus on Europe. *The Human Comedy* connects place references on six continents (all of them except Antarctica) through the stories and backstories of more than two thousand characters (Cerfberr and Christophe, 1902; Pugh, 1974). Indeed, it can be argued that *The Human Comedy* is the first series of novels with a truly global footprint that mentions cities, regions, and countries around the world in connection with its network of characters. These connections between characters and places often involve travel by merchants or soldiers in a story's recent past. Military characters like Colonel Chabert and Général Montriveau travel throughout Europe, Egypt, and Russia as a part of the Napoleonic army, returning to France to recount their stories after the wars. Merchants like Charles Grandet and Gobseck travel to Europe outside of France and to the West Indies, India, Malaysia, and European colonies. They travel to exploit natural resources and get rich trading in diamonds and spices, profiting from the emerging colonial connections between France and Asia, the Pacific, North Africa, and former colonies in the Caribbean and North America. Balzac's global geography is thus inextricably tied to war and colonization rather than to disinterested cosmopolitanism.

The global nature of Balzac's geography has often been ignored due to the omnipresence of Paris in Balzac criticism and the sheer volume of references to Paris in the text. There is little doubt that Balzac, himself no great traveler, was well versed in the obscure places of the world. The vastness of his erudition is well on display in allusions to African tribes, Chinese regions, and Eastern European towns. References to places from outside of Europe tend to be more abstract – to the West Indies ("les Indes"), the Orient ("l'Orient"), Central Asia ("la Tartarie"), and India ("les Grandes Indes"), rather than specific countries, regions, or towns. In a sense, Balzac's map of the world looks much as one would expect based on the balance of power in the nineteenth century: London, Rome, and Berlin figure prominently; China, Russia, and the Orient appear too, as do South America, the Antilles, and the eastern parts of North America. Compared to previous French literary geographies, Balzac's map of the world is far vaster and more reflective of the extent of French military and commercial connections in the early nineteenth century.

This section draws on the place references enumerated in the works of Balzac critics Léon-François Hoffman (Hoffman, 1965, 1968) and George Raser

(Raser, 1964). In order to produce maps, I have used geolocation services like Geohack in conjunction with encyclopedias of historical streets and gazetteers to add geographical coordinates to these place references. In some cases, I have also corrected errors and inaccuracies in attributions to places – for example, places that are listed as real when they were, in fact, fictional (e.g., "Frangistan"). I have also updated countries and regions to their current equivalents where the classifications were out of date (e.g., "Yugoslavia" or "Czechoslovakia" become their modern equivalents). Some cities are located in different countries than they were in the 1960s (e.g., "Riga"); in order to translate back and forth, I have retained both their name in Balzac (under "Raw place") and given the current equivalent (under "Modern place").

For places outside of France, my primary data source is Léon-François Hoffman's 1965 study, *Répertoire géographique de La Comédie humaine* (Hoffman 1965). In this study, Hoffman catalogs the mentions of "foreign" places – that is, places outside of France, or "l'Étranger" – in Balzac's series of novels and stories. Hoffman's study is invaluable because it is a manually created and logically organized list of place references in *The Human Comedy*, rather than a simple search for terms or strings, often called "tokens" in digital humanities. By categorizing place references by country and region, Hoffman organizes implicit references as well as explicit ones; for instance, in Hoffman's study, "Madrid" counts as a city and also as a reference to Spain. Another strength of Hoffman's method is that he excludes dead metaphors and words that no longer necessarily refer to the places that gave them their names, such as parmesan cheese ("parmesan") or Labrador dogs ("Labradors").[4] By excluding place words that are not active references to places and including implicit place references, Hoffman creates an ontology for place references in Balzac's fiction. He categorizes the various references at multiple levels (cities, countries, regions) so that, for example, Italian cities count as references to Italy and not only as particular municipalities. This system captures the implicit knowledge about how the world is laid out that readers usually bring to the text but that a computer lacks. Such explicitness is necessary in computational geography. Unless explicitly instructed that, for instance, Beijing is in China, or China is in Asia, a computer does not know about these semantic trees, since a computer does not have access to the kind of implicit cultural knowledge human readers have.

Figure 1 shows the places outside of France referenced in *The Human Comedy* as recorded by Hoffman. Each circle represents a place referenced,

---

[4] Hoffman also reviewed all of the references to remove synonyms (like the continent of Asia ["Asie"] and the woman's name "Asie," the alias of Jacqueline Collin, an important character in *The Splendors and Miseries of Courtesans*).

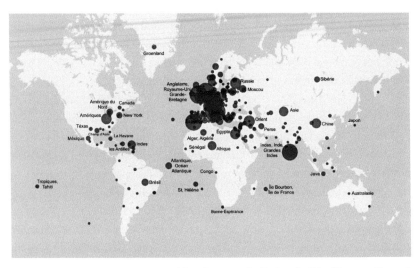

Figure 1 Referenced places outside of France in Balzac's *The Human Comedy*

and the circle is sized according to the number of references to that place in Balzac's series as a whole.

Figure 1 was produced in Palladio with a "streets" base map. In order for a textual place reference to appear on the map, latitude and longitude coordinates must be associated with the place. We can see several things in this diagram: the prominence in Balzac's geography of Western Europe and the areas around France, particularly Italy; the diversity of locales in Eastern and Northern Europe, which are nonetheless mentioned with a lesser frequency; finally, fewer references to places in Asia, the Americas, and Africa, particularly sub-Saharan Africa and the Pacific coast of both North and South America. Thus, despite the presence of many references to places on six continents, Balzac's geography is heavy with references to those countries that surround the Mediterranean and light on countries that are most distant from French imperial power, most notably the west coast of the Americas, southern Africa, and the Far East. This is the broadest view of Balzac's map of the world.

We cannot honestly discuss Balzac's geography, foreign or otherwise, without acknowledging the centrality of France. Undeniably, there are more references to places in France than there are to places outside of France in Balzac's work. Paris functions as a hub in this global network, with most of the characters passing through the city at one point; there are, therefore, far more references to Paris than to any other city. Table 1 shows the breakdown of place references in *The Human Comedy* according to Hoffman and Raser. Out of 14,861 place references in *The Human Comedy*, 4,860 are to places in Paris, 6,538 are to

Table 1 References to places by region in Balzac's *The Human Comedy*

Region	References to region	Distinct places referenced within region	Top book
Paris	4,860	786	*Splendors and Miseries*
Provinces	6,538	898	*The Chouans*
Outside of France	3,463	534	*On Catherine de Medici*
Total	14,861	2,218	

places in France outside of Paris, and 3,463 are to places outside of France (Table 1).

References to Paris, the provinces, and the rest of the world occur through almost all books in *The Human Comedy*. Rather than references being localized in one book or another, most books refer to places in Paris, the provinces, and the rest of the world. The constant comparison of places generated by countless interlocking references cuts against the geographical logic of a series of novels that foregrounds distinction and separation between Paris, the provinces, and elsewhere – with divisions like *Scenes from Parisian life*, *Scenes from Country Life*, and *Scenes from Military Life* that foreground contrasts between these spaces. While the toplines of this analysis hold, the presence of references to places in all three categories across all series undercuts the logic of division and replaces it with a logic of connection. Paris is by far the most connected city in *The Human Comedy*. The most connected foreign city is Venice, which appears in twenty-eight books. As a city, Paris remains the undisputed hub of the character networks and geography. The book with the most references to Paris, *The Splendors and Miseries of Courtesans*, is, unsurprisingly, both comparatively long and set in Paris. *The Chouans*, the fictionalized story of the Vendée rebellion, contains the most references to places in France outside of Paris, notably Brittany, where the novel is set. The historical narrative and essay *On Catherine de Medici* contains the most references to places outside of France, mainly to places in Italy.

The provinces receive a large plurality of Balzac's geographic mentions; there are several thousand more references to places in France but outside of Paris than to places either in Paris or outside of France. However, there are nearly as many distinct places referenced in Paris as in the provinces, and many more than in the rest of the world. Distinct places here can be specific streets, addresses, shops, or countries or regions; a reference to "Paris" counts as one distinct place, while the "Palais-Royal" is another, a specific shop or restaurant near the Palais-Royal another still. With 786 distinct places referenced in Paris, there is considerable detail in settings there compared to elsewhere, given the relatively small landmass of the French capital. Despite the much larger total number of references to places in France but outside of Paris, only slightly more distinct places are referenced there: 898 in the provinces, most of which are cities. Even fewer distinct places are referenced in the entire rest of the world (534), many of which are cities or regions and very few of which are addresses or buildings.

Returning to places outside of France (Figure 1), we see that the majority of foreign places mentioned in *The Human Comedy* are in Europe. There is a great deal of variation between books in the places mentioned, though all books mention some places in Europe. The regions surrounding France – notably England, the Germanic states, and parts of the Italian peninsula – are mentioned frequently; less so places in Asia or the Americas (Table 2).

Balzac's literary geography has been studied at length as a topic (his Orientalism, his blindness toward Africa, his views on the New World), yet literary cartographies of Balzac's place-names have focused on his detailed references to streets and houses in Paris more so than to Polynesian islands, the Antilles, China, Northern Europe, or Russia, all of which are referenced in multiple novels. We should not confuse mentioning a place with situating the action of a story in it or making that place central to the themes of the novel. The texts that mention the most distinct places do not necessarily set much action in or relate much detail about those places.

Table 2 References to places outside of France by continent in Balzac's *The Human Comedy*

Continent	References to continent	Distinct places referenced on continent	Number of books with references	Top book
Europe	2,676	358	85	*On Catherine de Medici*
Asia	491	84	68	*Letters of Two Brides*
Americas	205	48	50	*The Black Sheep*
Total	3,463	534	86	

In *On Catherine de Medici*, a historical essay on the life and influence of the Italian-born French queen of the Renaissance and later queen-regent of France, many of the references to foreign places are in fact references to political leaders and alliances, rather than plot points. Furthermore, as a historical, largely nonfictional digression, *On Catherine de Medici* is atypical of texts in *The Human Comedy*.

As we have seen, Balzac's map of the world reflects both his status as a French writer and the balance of power in the nineteenth century, with great emphasis given to major European cities near France, less emphasis given to the rest of Eurasia, and even less mention of the Americas. In order to analyze these patterns, we will examine the frequency of references to countries and similar regions outside of France (Table 3).

These numbers, and in particular the interplay between references to a country and the number of distinct places referenced within that country, provide some counterevidence to the idea that Balzac saw the world in broad strokes, perceiving few distinctions within the likes of Russia, the Middle East, and Asia. Graham Robb writes, "Beyond Western Europe, Balzac's geography was like an ancient map; Russia to him was part of the mysterious Orient" (Robb, 1995, p. 229). There is, indeed, wide variability in the importance of individual places in Balzac's work. However, the relationship between proximity to France and abstraction is not so simple as to say that greater distance equals increasing abstraction. Balzac mentions cities and small towns in Eastern Europe, the Americas, Africa, and Asia. Some European countries like Great Britain and Spain are referenced hundreds of times, but distinct locales within these countries merit only a handful of mentions. By contrast, particular places within Egypt are mentioned almost as often as distinct places in Great Britain and Spain, even though Egypt as a country is mentioned less frequently. Thus, it is Great Britain and Spain that mainly appear as abstractions, such as in generalizations about their peoples and cultures, while references to Egypt are more often particularized. Even broader locations like "the New World," "Africa," or the "Orient" gesture toward places on the world map that are complemented by precise locations like "Sharonville" (Ohio), "Sinai" (Egypt), Niger, Madagascar, Khiva, Kashmir, Lahore, etc. The single most challenging set of places to localize is the "Indes," "Grandes Indes," or "Inde," which sometimes refers only to the country of India, sometimes to the East Indies generally, sometimes only to the West Indies, and sometimes to both the East and West Indies. For this reason, these references are divided between what is now India and what is now the Caribbean.

Table 3 References to countries outside of France in Balzac's *The Human Comedy*

Country	References to country	Distinct places referenced within country	Number of books with references	Top book
Italian states	714	80	71	*Massimilla Doni*
Germanic states	301	59	57	*The Red Inn*
Great Britain	272	19	61	*The Lily of the Valley*
Spain	214	22	44	*Splendors and Miseries*
Switzerland	176	32	41	*Albert Savarus*
Russia	141	13	36	*The Country Doctor*
Belgium	130	23	42	*The Quest of the Absolute*
Egypt	68	14	25	*The Country Doctor*
Orient	57	N/A[a]	30	*The Physiology of Marriage*
World Total	3,463	535	86	

[a] Due to the amorphous nature of the "Orient," I do not count distinct places within the Orient but only explicit references to that region. Distinct places within the Middle East and Asia are instead categorized according to the modern country in which the place occurs, such as "Egypt," "China," "Israel," or "Syria." While this system is not perfect, it accounts for most distinct places, as almost all references are to historical places that still exist. Some exceptions include "Persia," rather than Iran, since Balzac uses that term frequently, and the Indies, which cannot always be precisely localized or tied to one modern region.

References to cities, towns, and battle sites (Table 4) follow a similar pattern, extending throughout the world but concentrated in Europe. The eleven most-referenced cities in *The Human Comedy* are all in Europe. One of the only

Table 4 Most-referenced cities / towns / battle sites in Balzac's *The Human Comedy*

City / town / battle site	References to location	Books with references	Top book	Associated characters[a]
Venice	108	28	*Massimilla Doni*	Facino Cane; Emilio Cane; Massimilla Doni; Gambara; La Palférine
Rome	90	42	*Sarrasine / On Catherine de Medici*	Camille Maupin; Cousin Pons; del Pimbo; Sarrasine; Séraphitüs; Raphaël de Valentin
London	80	35	*Séraphíta*	Baron de Séraphitüs; Castanier; Facino Cane; Canalis; Elie Magnus; Z. Marcus
Florence	40	14	*On Catherine de Medici*	Camille Maupin; Thadée Paz; Lucien de Rubempré; Bandello
Waterloo	35	20	*The Country Doctor*	Genestas; Luigi di Porta; Philippe Bridau; Paul de Manerville; Charles Mignon; Baron Hulot
Milan	33	18	*Albert Savarus*	Albert Savarus; La Marana; the Montefiore; Francesca d'Argaiolo
Naples	27	19	*Albert Savarus*	Castanier; Nucingen; Delphine de Nucingen
Vienna	23	20	*Cousin Pons / The Country Doctor*	Charles de Vandenesse; Duc d'Hérouville; father of La Palférine; Z. Marcas
Stromfiord*	23	1	*Séraphíta*	Séraphíta

* *indicates fictional location*

[a] Selected associated characters, including those with the most ties with the place and central characters.

fictional places outside of France described at length in *The Human Comedy* is the inlet of Stromfiord in Norway, located halfway between Trondhjem and Christiansand, according to *Séraphîta*, the only text in which the region appears. Balzac describes the layout, geology, history, and other aspects of the fiord and of Jarvis, the small town of around two hundred houses north of the inlet. Balzac uses the same techniques he employs to describe French towns and villages to depict Stromfiord, Jarvis, and their environs visually, culturally, and geographically, placing them within a cartographical visual space and a vista that the narrator describes in detail from his own visual perspective. Balzac regularly pays attention to the interaction of culture, place, and characters; he most often does so within historical frameworks, no matter how stereotypical.

Many of these frequently referenced locations are Italian cities (Rome, Venice, and Florence) or the sites of Napoleonic battles (Waterloo, Moscow, Berezina, Austerlitz). As we shall see, most of these references are to settings in the near past that appear throughout *The Human Comedy*, in plots or subplots set during the Napoleonic Wars. No historical period weighs more heavily on the foreign geography of *The Human Comedy* than the Napoleonic Wars. Many of the contacts between Parisian characters and the outside world are due to military conflicts during the lives of the fathers and grandfathers of the primary characters. From Moscow to North Africa, wars explain many of the movements of characters; they also explain the deaths of young men far from Paris, interludes away from Paris, and changes in the social status of characters who participate in or benefit from imperial wars. The military elements of Balzac's map of the world exemplify one of the contradictory aspects of Balzac's global network of characters. The military characters of *The Human Comedy* are far more likely than nonmilitary characters to have contact with people from other countries, but along with this contact come violence, disease, and exposure to unfamiliar environments, which significantly raise their mortality rate. More central to the global network than nonmilitary members of their social milieu, the soldiers are exposed to the good and bad of foreign contacts: financial gain as well as personal loss, death and injury, but also adventures beyond what was possible in metropolitan France. They lead high-risk lives that sometimes bring large rewards but more often end in tragedy.

The geographical core of *The Human Comedy* is largely coextensive with the First French Empire at its height. Many of the small towns and sites like Berezina and Austerlitz appear only in reference to battles and the movement of Napoleonic troops. Indeed, Balzac's map of the world outside of Western Europe is, for the most part, coextensive with the movements of French troops during the Napoleonic Wars and, later, the early colonization of North Africa. Although he does not glorify the wars of the era, Balzac does pay greater attention to those areas of the world at war with France, or those areas invaded and colonized by the French. Balzac's map of the world also anticipates further expansions of the Empire into Africa and Asia. Still, Paris is the undisputed center of this map: the secondary sites radiate out from Paris; close-in Mediterranean locations from Italy to Greece to Egypt account for most of the foreign references. Even within this central space, there are areas and regions that are more favored than others. In the case of Algeria, for example, Balzac paints Algiers and its environs as the place for Europeans to meet an early death or lose a fortune. "Balzac was never interested in Algeria as anything" but "a colony," as Dorian Bell has argued, and that is why the "lives and body parts cut short" of the young men who do a short stint there "evoke the status in the *Comédie Humaine* of Algeria itself" (Bell, 2011, p. 35). Philippe Bridau and Johann Fischer lose their lives there, the former decapitated and the latter a suicide; Oscar Husson loses an arm. In *The Human Comedy*, Algeria and other colonies are dangerous places defined by their impact on traders and colonial powers. Unlike Berezina, the disastrous end of the Russian campaign depicted in *Adieu*, Algeria is never a primary setting in *The Human Comedy* and is consigned to backstory in all of the completed stories. We can see, thus, that the inclusion of a place within Balzac's literary geography does not guarantee an interest in the people who live there or the independent history of that place, but often serves to underscore the preeminence of Europe, France, and Paris.

2.3 Balzac's Paris As a Hub

What does it mean to be the hub of a global network? It does not mean Paris was the only hub, or the only possible hub. Parisians were, however, more likely to have roots in the French provinces or other European countries than were the inhabitants of other possible hubs, meaning almost all characters in the series are connected to Paris at one point in their lives. Balzac's character network reflects this dominance of Paris in the cultural economy of post-1789 Europe. Paris is by far the most-referenced city in *The Human Comedy*, appearing in almost all of the books and in relation to the largest number of characters. It is the most common primary setting and at the heart of the character-place network of the fictional world. While there are more references to places outside of Paris than to places in the French capital, the level of detail within the region of Île-de-France goes well beyond what appears even in other regional capitals that serve as primary settings for Balzac's fiction. Balzac includes all major regions in central Paris and much of Île-de-France in his geography (Guichardet, 1986). Figure 2 shows the places referenced in Balzac's Paris in *The Human Comedy*.

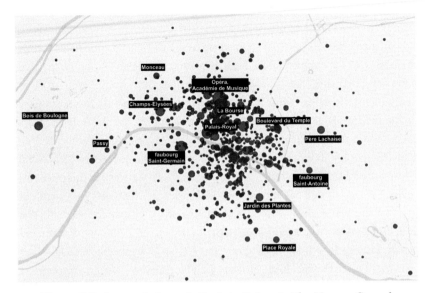

Figure 2 Referenced places in Paris in Balzac's *The Human Comedy*

Balzac's Paris has a rigid class structure in the sense that one's address says a great deal about how much money one has, where one comes from, and, all too often, where one is going. Nevertheless, Balzac delights in the open public spaces where people of different classes with their varying *moeurs* clash. At first glance, Balzac's Paris is split between high- and low-status areas, especially the aristocratic faubourg Saint-Germain and the Latin Quarter. The faubourg Saint-Germain is the epicenter of aristocratic residences, the *hôtels particuliers* of fashionable ladies, which many characters seek to enter. The Latin Quarter is the haunt of young students, the starting point for many of their adventures. Not in itself low in status or impoverished, the Latin Quarter is only coded as "low" in Balzac's work since many of his protagonists (e.g., Lucien de Rubempré, Rastignac, d'Arthèz) aspire to leave it and find a *hôtel* in a more fashionable district. Critics have frequently identified these two quartiers as the two poles of Balzac's Paris, which is organized along these principal axes as an imaginary climb from the lower quarters to the higher ones, with potential falls into the lower depths (*bas-fonds*). Both of these quartiers loom large in the imaginary geography of *The Human Comedy* – not least because Balzac mentions both of them explicitly many times. In all of *The Human Comedy*, the faubourg Saint-Germain appears explicitly 117 times (either as the "faubourg Saint-Germain" or as the "faubourg"), while the Latin Quarter appears only 9 times (Figure 2). The Sorbonne, for all of its fame as a setting for *Lost Illusions* and other semi-autobiographical books, is only mentioned 9 times, as is the rue de Cluny.

Indeed, the right bank and Île de la Cité far outweigh the Latin Quarter as settings and points of reference, as do other areas on the left bank. Other binaries could be said to structure areas of the city in apparent oppositions. Franco Moretti has mapped Lucien's helpers and antagonists; he discovered that the antagonists are disproportionately in or near the Saint-Germain, and his helpers are located in the Latin Quarter or across the Seine, especially near the Boulevard du Temple (Moretti, 1999, p. 69). These friend/foe relations are built on class differences and the socioeconomic gaps between neighborhoods.

Unsurprisingly, places near the populous center of the city are more numerous and more frequently referred to than places on the periphery. The Bois de Boulogne, mentioned 57 times, marks what could be considered the western limit of the city before reaching the numerous smaller suburbs (Versailles, Neuilly, Boulogne-Billancourt, etc.) to the west of the capital, most of which were relatively wealthy in Balzac's time, as they are today. The Bois de Vincennes, mentioned 11 times, marks the eastern boundary of the city. Aside from a few references to Saint-Denis and Poissy prison to the northeast, the northern boundary of Balzac's Paris is marked by Montmartre (16 references) and environs. By far the highest density of place references lies along the Seine, on the right bank, especially in the area around the Louvre and the Tuileries Palace, as well as the opera and theater districts. The places referenced the most are L'Opéra (155), the faubourg Saint-Germain (117), the Tuileries (117), the Théâtre-Italien (85), Palais-Royal (81), the Conciergerie (72), the Champs-Élysées (59), the rue Saint-Honoré (52), and the Louvre (51). These places are distributed throughout the city, but they are disproportionately connected to the centers of royal power: the Louvre, the Tuileries, and Châtelet (22). Many of the most-referenced places are palaces or former palaces like the Conciergerie, a gothic palace on the Île de la Cité that was a prison in the nineteenth century, or the Louvre, which had recently become a museum. Despite Balzac's self-description as a conservative Catholic, relatively few churches are referenced, and those referenced are not mentioned very frequently. Even Notre-Dame is only mentioned 25 times, nowhere near as many times as the theaters or important streets like the rue Saint-Denis. In many of these references, these places are used as place-markers in phrases such as "near the Tuileries" and not precise locations. In effect, they are places that would be known to people who do not live in Paris as well as to Parisians and thus are referenced in part because they are already famous. Some of these historic places, notably the Palais-Royal, with its walking paths, shops, and restaurants, frequently serve as a setting.

As Raser points out, Balzac focuses not on the high or low Paris but the places where high and low meet: the boulevards, arcades, theaters, opera houses, and promenades where a duchess might encounter a young man from the provinces (Rascr, 1970, p. 16). The Palais-Royal is exemplary of these spaces of encounter where anyone could meet and seemingly anything could happen.

The Palais-Royal in the late eighteenth and early nineteenth centuries brought together a number of commercial activities from theater to restaurants to prostitution. Associated with, and at one time owned by, the Orléans branch of the French royal family, the Palais-Royal was directly across the street from the stock market, or Bourse, recently reopened by Napoleon after it had been closed under the Ancien Régime, and also near the Théâtre Français, today known as the Comédie Française. The Palais-Royal brought opposites together under the unifying aegis of capitalism. *Lost Illusions* provides perhaps the most exemplary description of the class-melding function of the Palais-Royal as Lucien Chardon arrives in the wooden galleries through the Galerie d'Orléans, which the narrator calls a "flowerless hothouse," and travels through the series of galleries the narrator refers to as "one of the most famous sights of Paris" (*CH*, vol. VIII, p. 211). In *Lost Illusions*, the Palais-Royal introduces Lucien to the capitalistic world of book publishing as he encounters the rapacious and miserly booksellers Ladvocat and Dauriat, who, he will come to realize, dominate the Parisian literary world. It is worth noting that this experience is immediately preceded by a description of high-class men and prostitutes, a metaphor Balzac later develops for writers seeking to earn a living. This *galerie* is a meeting of laughter and horror, joy and sadness, dark and light, elegance and depravity:

> La licence des interrogations et des réponses, ce cynisme public en harmonie avec le lieu ne se retrouve plus, ni au bal masqué, ni dans les bals si célèbres qui se donnent aujourd'hui ... La chair éclatante des épaules et des gorges étincelait au milieu des vêtements d'hommes presque toujours sombres, et produisait les plus magnifiques oppositions. (*CH*, vol. VIII, pp. 215–216)

> The freewheeling questions and answers, a public cynicism in harmony with the place – these are no longer found, neither at the masked ball nor in the famous balls thrown today ... The radiant flesh of shoulders and throats shone amidst the men's habitually dark clothes, creating the most magnificent contrasts.

An engraving by an unknown artist provides a view of this part of the Palais-Royal Galerie Montpensier and the Galerie de Beaujolais in 1800 (Figure 3). We can see the dramatic clash between feminine and masculine styles, rich and carefree, poor and struggling, in the Palais-Royal that captivated Balzac and to which he returned again and again as a microcosm of Paris as a whole, a meeting point for all – notably in *The Splendors and Miseries of Courtesans*.

Figure 3 Galeries du Palais-Royal. Courtesy of the Bibliothèque Nationale de France

Despite the dominance of aristocratic and even royal places in the list of most mentioned places, when we consider the overall number of references to places in a quarter and not just the most famous ones, we see that the petite bourgeoisie and the grande bourgeoisie are quite dominant. We can see the underlying class logic in Balzac's Paris thanks to Raser's organization of the data by category according to the dominant class in that region in the city (Table 5). In order to make the logic of these references clearer, Raser organizes the places referenced into groups of quarters. Table 5 shows the most referenced of Raser's groups of quarters, organized from those that have the most references to those that have the least. Unsurprisingly, the central quarters are referenced more than the outer quarters, as well as having more distinct referenced places.[5]

The most-referenced districts actually overlap, since the quarters of the small tradespeople, the boulevards, and the theaters are all right-bank districts centered around rue Saint-Denis to the rue Saint-Martin. Unsurprisingly, the top

---

[5] These numbers are lower than the total numbers in Raser's study because he includes places mentioned in Balzac's *Correspondence*, *Enseignes de Paris*, texts published in the *Revue de Paris*, and others that I have labeled *Oeuvres diverses* or *Oeuvres de jeunesse*. I include only the place references in *The Human Comedy*. I have also excluded vehicles and other textual references that cannot be localized

Table 5 Place references by district in Paris in Balzac's *Human Comedy*

Quarter or district	References to district	Distinct places referenced in district	Number of books with references	Top book
The Small Tradespeople	627	134	54	*César Birotteau*
The Richer Bourgeoisie	614	110	67	*Cousin Betty*
The Theaters	557	33	67	*Lost Illusions*
The Boulevards	426	102	53	*Lost Illusions*
Latin Quarter	373	82	50	*Lost Illusions*
The Financial Quarter	352	61	53	*Splendors and Miseries*
La Cité	350	70	40	*Splendors and Miseries*
Outer Right-Bank Faubourgs	340	61	55	*Splendors and Miseries*
Faubourg Saint-Germain	294	38	45	*Cousin Betty*
Left-Bank Districts of Poverty and Indigence	194	39	36	*Old Man Goriot*
Total	4,648[a]	806	88	

[a] These totals include other districts with fewer place references. Raser divides Paris into fourteen regions.

book for the small tradespeople is *César Birotteau*, the story of an enterprising perfumer ruined by extravagance as he tries to enter high society by overspending on furnishings, clothes, jewelry, food, and other luxuries for his spendthrift wife and daughter, whom he hopes to marry off to a wealthy suitor, having proved his worth for dignified employment. But Balzac's Paris does not totally obey the segmenting logic of quarters: in fact, he overrepresents places where class mixing is more common (e.g., theaters, boulevards, promenades) and he underrepresents residential areas that are more segregated (e.g., churches, schools, and residential districts). Indeed, the protagonists' residences often mark a place where a character is *stuck*, whether in a poor boarding house or the family home, and not a place where one can potentially start an adventure or find a new life like a theater, a boulevard, a shop, or a grand apartment of a society woman.

From a purely technical perspective, the literary cartography of Balzac's Paris is the most challenging in this Element. Whereas the places Balzac refers to in the rest of France and the world tend to be cities or countries, Balzac often refers to particular streets or even shops and restaurants in his descriptions of Paris locations. Balzac's Paris is a pre-Haussmannization Paris of smaller streets and local neighborhoods before boulevards had cut through the capital (see Figure 4). Some streets are easy to find; others are all but impossible. Obviously, few of the shops and restaurants he refers to are open in the present day and, thus, geolocating them means finding their original address, figuring out which street now occupies that space, and then finding an approximate location on the current

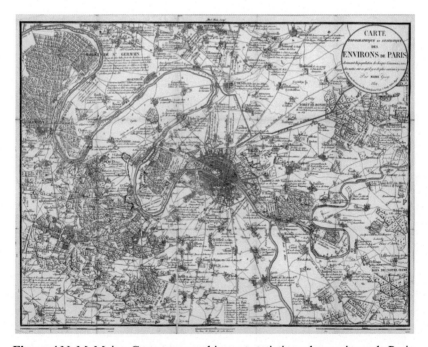

Figure 4 N. M. Maire. Carte topographique et statistique des environs de Paris. Courtesy of the David Rumsey Map collection

street. If the building happens to be located at the intersection of two localizable streets, the resulting geolocation can be very accurate, to within a few tens of meters, but if the location is only known to be somewhere along some street or avenue, the margin of error is considerably greater. Thankfully historians and amateurs have been pursuing research on changes in Paris for centuries, and the older names and locations are often preserved and presented in dictionaries of streets that can be used to convert an older address to a modern one.

Many complications arise when analyzing historical data with current digital tools. One complication is that many locations may be gone or streets renamed. Some of the *hôtels particuliers* are fictional, some of them are historical, and some of them mix the name of a well-known house with the location of a different residence. Further, the character of some neighborhoods has changed radically in the present day, including the Marais (fifty references), formerly very conservative and now very trendy, and Montmartre, which was sleepy before the construction of Sacré-Coeur and is now overrun by tourists most of the year. Balzac's Paris is interesting in part because it is so different from the Paris of today. The author has preserved the sights and smells of a pre-Haussmann Paris with its small streets and less frequent movement between neighborhoods. He and other nineteenth-century novelists evoke a Paris without the metro that nevertheless had forms of semi-regular, semipublic transportation like the omnibus (Belenky, 2020). The kinds of transport Balzac describes as available within the capital are a subject of much critical discussion; these varying modes of travel influence the travel time between neighborhoods. The metro and train system has made the Bois de Boulogne, Vincennes, and Versailles seem close to one another, whereas they would have been quite a journey on foot or in a carriage; further, the train permitted ever more rapid travel from Paris to almost all parts of France (Bell, 2010). We cannot, therefore, immediately draw conclusions about the accessibility of points or travel times from distances alone. Nor can we assume that places that are densely populated today were likewise in the 1830s. These difficulties in seeing how the historical, the fictional, and present-day realities overlap are all the more present because many tools like Google Maps do not make affordances for historical data. Thus, it is necessary to make frequent comparisons between historical and contemporary maps and descriptions when using mapmaking tools.

2.4 Balzac's Provinces and the Emerging French Nation

Balzac was one of the first French writers to make use of French geography on a national scale. Other writers had focused on particular regions or the contrast between Paris and the provinces. The early modern period had numerous cartographically inspired writers (Conley, 1996). Balzac was the first, or at least one of the first, to register in literary form the complexity of the geography of the French provinces and their inhabitants on a national scale. Many of Balzac's descriptions of individual provinces are incorrect or biased (Robb, 2008, pp. 153–154), but they are often some of the first representations of those regions in best-selling books. As Ferdinand Brunetière writes:

> Cherchez en effet, et, si vous le pouvez, mesurez dans l'oeuvre des prédécesseurs de Balzac la place qu'y occupait la province. Elle est nulle, pour ainsi dire, et nos romans français du XVIIIe siècle ne sont jamais 'localisés' qu'à Paris ou à l'étranger, dans l'Espagne de Le Sage, ou dans l'Angleterre de l'abbé Prévost. Mais, dans l'œuvre de Balzac, il a raison de le dire, c'est toute une 'géographie de la France'. (97–98)

> Go and look amongst the works of Balzac's predecessors and, if you can, measure how much of them is occupied with the provinces. The answer is none, to state it plainly, and our French novels of the eighteenth century are never "localized" except in Paris or abroad, as in Le Sage's Spain or Abbé Prévost's England. But Balzac is right to say his works contain an entire "geography of France."

For Brunetière, geography, rather than social relations, constitutes *The Human Comedy*'s principal historical value ("valeur historique") (98). Balzac himself emphasizes the national character of his geography over its Parisian and global portions. No doubt integrating this range of French locales involved a great deal of research, including visits, often by train, to sites described in the work. Nevertheless, there is also a great deal of imagination and conjecture in Balzac's provincial locations. Where Balzac really breaks with his predecessors is in his descriptions of geographical particulars:

> Plusieurs de ses descriptions de villes et de provinces sont-elles justement demeurées célèbres, comme la description de la petite ville de Guérande, par exemple, dans *Béatrix,* ou celle du pays de Fougères, dans *les Chouans*. (98)

> Several of his descriptions of towns and provinces have justly remained famous, such as that of the small town of Guérande in *Béatrix*, for example, or of the countryside of Fougères, in *The Chouans*.

A similar critical discussion has taken place around other provincial towns in Balzac's work – Tours, Angoulême, Saumur (the site of Grandet's house in *Eugénie Grandet*) – in which some elements, often buildings associated with the main characters, are fictionalized and others, most often the name of the town and monuments like castles, are historical. It is hard to determine exactly how much Balzac knew about some of these towns or why he decided to fictionalize parts of their layout. By mapping Balzac's provincial geograph-ical references, we can see which areas are most central to his national geography and which places do not occupy Balzac's imaginary. Figure 5 shows historical places referenced in *The Human Comedy*. As Brunetière notes, Brittany plays an outsized role, as do many locations surrounding Paris, including Versailles (64), the Seine (35), Saint-Denis (19), Vincennes (17), and Charenton (14). A bit further out are Nemours (89), Champagne (24), and the Avonne river (22). The north is well represented, with Normandie (78), Le Havre (60), Rouen (23), and other northern locations appearing frequently. The Midi (16) and the southeast are underrepresented, with Provence (40) having the highest number of references and other major population centers like Marseille (30), Nice (5), and Montpellier (2) men-tioned only occasionally. The Mediterranean as a body of water is mentioned 14 times. The Savoy region as a whole merits 19 mentions, while Lyon gets 25 and Grenoble 28. Toulon, the primary military port in France, appears 15 times, much more than would be expected based solely on its population at the time or its cultural significance.

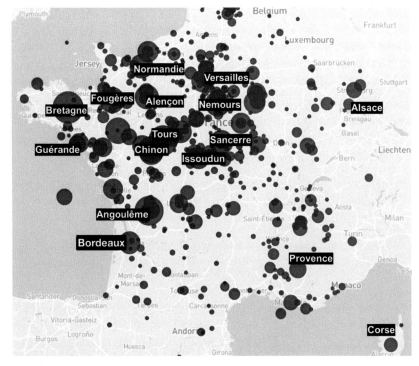

Figure 5 Referenced historical places in France (outside of Paris) in Balzac's
The Human Comedy

The most-referenced single place outside of Paris is Brittany ["la Bretagne"] (144). Within Brittany, a small town of particular interest to Balzac is Fougères; along with its associated sites, including the Château de Fougères and the Eglise Saint-Suplice, Fougères is mentioned 93 times. Nantes, still considered part of Brittany in Balzac's day, is mentioned 49 times, but other major cities in Brittany get few mentions, including Brest (9) and Rennes (2). Balzac's description of Fougères is justly famous for its invocation of the landscape and the castle that towers over the rocks, as three battalions of royalist troops, one from Fougères, view the town on the horizon.

> Du sommet de La Pellerine apparaît aux yeux du voyageur la grande vallée du Couesnon, dont l'un des points culminants est occupé à l'horizon par la ville de Fougères. Son château domine, en haut du rocher où il est bâti, trois au quatre routes importantes, position qui la rendait jadis une des clés de la Bretagne. (*CH*, vol. XIV, p. 8)

> From the summit of La Pellerine appears to the eyes of the traveler the great valley of Couesnon, one of whose highest points is occupied at the horizon by the town of Fougères. Its castle, atop the rock where it is built, dominates three or four important roads, a position which once made it one of the keys to Brittany.

The soldiers are stunned by the view, not because it is unfamiliar but because they know it all too well and are nevertheless overcome by the natural beauty of the rock and the harmonization of the architecture with the natural setting.

> Quoiqu'ils vinssent de Fougères, où le tableau qui se présentait alors à leurs yeux se voit également, mais avec les différences que le changement de perspective lui fait subir, ils ne purent se refuser à l'admirer une dernière fois, semblables à ces dilettanti auxquels une musique donne d'autant plus de jouissances qu'ils en connaissent mieux les details. (*CH*, vol. XIV, p. 8)

> Even though they came from Fougères, where the panorama which then presented itself to their eyes can also be seen, though with the differences that a change of perspective imposes, they could not begrudge admiring it one last time, like those dilettantes for whom a song gives all the more pleasure the better they know its details.

Another region very strongly overrepresented based on the population of the time is the Val du Loire, or Loire Valley, from Orléans (29) to Blois (68), including Balzac's native Tours (98) located in Touraine (80). The Loire itself is mentioned 95 times. Balzac does have considerable reach beyond these main settings of his novels. He describes many places in the east, including Strasbourg (33), Nancy (8), and Metz (5). The Alsace region is named 15 times, while Lorraine gets 8 mentions. Balzac describes few places in the Pyrenees and along the Spanish border. The Pyrenees themselves are mentioned by name a total of 7 times, while the department of Pyrénées-Orientales gets 2 mentions. Within that department, the town of Mont-Louis gets a single mention; likewise, the town of Barèges in the department of Hautes-Pyrénées. The province of Béarn is noted 7 times, while the city of Bayonne, at the southwestern tip of France, gets 3 mentions.

Figure 6 shows the references to fictional places in the provinces in *The Human Comedy*. It should be noted that some fictional places, in particular *terres* said to belong to fictional families, are either difficult to geolocate or cannot be geolocated at all. However, many of the fictional places are described as near a historical location or near a larger town that permits us to guess at an approximate location. Still, most of the references to places in the provinces are historical (5,643) rather than fictional (840), so locating this smaller number of nonhistorical places is made easier by the large number of places that appear on existing maps.

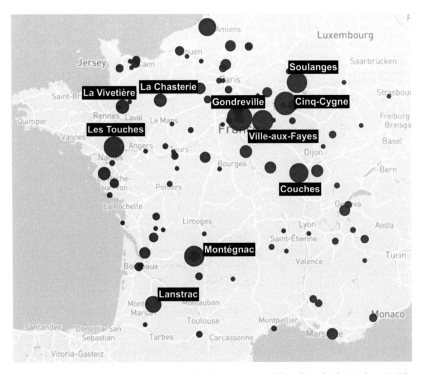

Figure 6 Referenced fictional places in France (outside of Paris) in Balzac's *The Human Comedy*

Of Balzac's fictional places in the provinces, Gondreville (69), Ville-aux-Fayes (53), Cinq-Cygne (55), Montégnac (43), and Les Touches (45) appear the most (Figure 6). Cinq-Cygne and Gondreville both appear in *A Murky Business* ["*Une ténébreuse affaire*"], sometimes translated as *The Gondreville Mystery*, as well as *The Deputy of Arcis*, an unfinished novel set in the same general area near Troyes. Like many country homes, Cinq-Cygne is introduced in primarily genealogical terms with a great deal of interest paid to the previous owners of the land and the legacy of the property:

> Ce courtisan, repoussé du Louvre, avait épousé la veuve du comte de Cinq-Cygne, la branche cadette de la fameuse maison de Chargeboeuf, une des plus illustres de la vieille comté de Champagne, mais qui devint aussi célèbre et plus opulente que l'aînée. Le marquis, un des hommes les plus riches de ce temps, au lieu de se ruiner à la cour, bâtit Gondreville, en composa les domaines, et y joignit des terres, uniquement pour se faire une belle chasse. (*CH*, vol. XII, p. 229)

> This courtier, repelled from the Louvre, had married the widow of the Count of Cinq-Cygne, the younger branch of the famous house of Chargeboeuf, one of the most illustrious in the old county of Champagne, but which became as famous and more opulent than the elder branch. The marquis, one of the richest men of that time, rather than ruining himself at court, built Gondreville, developed the estate, and added land to it, solely to prepare for himself a good hunt.

We further learn that this courtier also built the Hôtel de Simeuse near the Hôtel de Cinq-Cygne and that these were two of the few stone houses in Troyes. The Marquis eventually sold Simeuse to the Duke of Lorraine. All this back-story is emblematic of the way Balzac uses fictional ancestral lands throughout *The Human Comedy*.

Beyond the descriptions of individual villages and landscapes, *The Human Comedy* introduces an understanding of the provinces as essential to the life of France. How can we compare that portrait to something in the historical record that might give us a sense of the particularities of Balzac's provinces? I suggest that looking at the absences in Balzac's map of France can be more enlightening than looking at those regions he depicts, not least because he presents such a broad view of the country.

Figure 7 is a nineteenth-century population density map by the French Ministry of the Interior, which shows the French departments colored lighter for lower population density and darker for higher population density. Such experiments in information visualization were relatively new in the nine-teenth century, especially the use of mapping to depict concepts in human geography such as population density. These sociological forms of mapping

Figure 7 Population density of French departments. Nineteenth century.
[Densité de la population, Ministère de l'Intérieur]. Courtesy of the David
Rumsey Map Collection

complemented the older tradition of physical geography and the associated
cartographical traditions. Yet such maps were rare, and the series on population, literacy rates, alcohol consumption, and other data of potential sociological interest of which this map is a part is a rare use of color to present
sociological data in this period. The map bears a legend that shows that the
Seine, meaning the Paris region, has a population density of more than 5,000
people per square kilometer. These numbers are higher than they would have
been in Balzac's day since the map was produced in 1881 and presents data
from the then most recent census. Nevertheless, this does give us a general
idea of which departments were the most populous in the nineteenth century.
The first range of data is from 20 to 39 people per square kilometer. The only
departments that had a population that low were Corsica, Landes in the west,
Lozère in the Midi, and the Hautes et Basses Alpes. The next range from 40
to 59 people per square kilometer covers much of what is today the Grand
Est, the Loire Valley, the Spanish border, and parts of the Alps, including
Savoy. The following two ranges are from 60 to 79 and then from 80 to 99

people per square kilometer, and they cover much of the Atlantic coast, Brittany, the border with Germany, and the areas around Lyon. Finally, we have ranges from 100 to 199 and 200 to 300; these ranges cover the Seine and Oise departments surrounding Paris, the Seine-Inférieure, Lyon proper and its department of the Rhône, as well as the adjoining Loire department and Marseille, or the Bouches-du-Rhône.

Comparing the maps of textual mentions of places in Balzac's *The Human Comedy*, we can get an inexact sense of which departments might be underrepresented in Balzac compared to their population and cultural weight, not in the interests of "correcting" Balzac's geography but in order to see which historical places are of lesser interest to him. We can see that Balzac's interest in Brittany and the Atlantic coast generally is not surprising given the population trends. So too is his inclusion of places like Charente, and his lack of representations of occupied places along the Spanish border and in the Alps makes sense from the perspective of population density. However, Touraine and the area between Paris and Touraine are much less populated than one might imagine based on Balzac's work. Conversely, Marseille and Lyon very much stick out as heavily populated urban areas that do not draw his interest. The lack of references to Marseilles is notable given that city's importance in population, economic production, and political matters; so too with Lyon, another center of industrial life in nineteenth-century France, notably textile production. The underrepresentation of urban centers like Marseille and Lyon may signal a lack of interest in their local cultures. It may also be a way of highlighting contrasts between Paris and the provinces by downplaying other urban centers. Either way, a strictly historical project, which *The Human Comedy* certainly is not, would include more on these rival locations of urban life in France – two cities which are indeed known for their working-class and industrial populations at a time when the working classes were becoming more dominant.

We can see that Balzac's sociological interest broadly tracks with the population in France, with exaggerated emphasis on his native Touraine and the Loire Valley, home of many of France's royal chateaux. The prominence of places within a train's ride from Paris perhaps contributes to the polarized effect of Paris versus the provinces in Balzac, the other large cities being de-emphasized and rural areas near Paris being more central than what would be generally expected.

The Human Comedy consists of ad hoc categories that bring together texts of widely divergent lengths and even genres. In some cases, they contain a large number of unrelated texts, and the groupings themselves were created after the fact to add structure to Balzac's magnum opus. Whereas *Scenes from Private Life* contains twenty-four different novels and short stories, *Analytical Studies* contains only three essays, which explains the small number of geographical references in those texts. Bearing in mind these differences, it remains interesting to look at the rough proportions of place references within each series. Unsurprisingly, *Scenes from a Provincial Life* contains a very large number of references to places in the provinces and a much smaller number of references to places in Paris or the world. Conversely, *Scenes from Parisian Life* contains a high number of references to places in Paris as well as the world and, to a lesser extent, the provinces. The number of place references in *Philosophical Studies* is high, primarily due to the presence of *On Catherine de Medici*, the historical essay on the life of the French queen.

So, while there are patterns in the distribution of place references across series, the fact remains that there are a large number of references to Paris in the provincial series and to the provinces in the "Parisian" stories. *The Human Comedy* creates connections across these series through the many characters moving from the provinces to Paris and back, through the many analogies to other places, and through quasi-sociological comparisons between Parisian societies and those of other cities and towns in France.

2.5 Time and Networks in *The Human Comedy*

The meaning of Balzac's *The Human Comedy* obviously amounts to more than a catalog of which places are referred to, visited, or experienced. Visualizations alone cannot replace the reading of the text, but they can identify broad patterns, some of which may not be apparent to a casual reader of the text. In this section, I show how to create visualizations like bubblelines and network graphs that show how places are connected to characters and time sequences. These tools permit researchers to explore geographical data in ever more sophisticated ways not available to earlier generations of scholars. By using network graphs to map the places associated with characters, we can see the conceptual structure of connections between characters and places, rather than their physical location. In the case of *The Human Comedy*, we see that the types of characters who are mobile between Paris and the provinces are younger and more ambitious than other characters, a cliché of Balzac studies. More surprisingly, characters connected to foreign places are either foreign-born themselves or of an older generation. Looking at these patterns together, we can see that Balzac's view of the foreign is not merely anthropological but also proto-colonialist with an emphasis on war and commerce, including the most exploitative forms of capitalism and slave trading associated with the Antilles and the French presence there, an emerging theme for the French novel (Prasad, 2003). Within France, the temporal arrangement of place references in Balzac is highly correlated with the setting, but references to foreign places are more aligned with the gender, age, and professional traits of characters.

The most common way to represent geographical data is via a map with overlaid data. It is essential to remember that maps are not the only way to represent geographical information, and just because places *can* be shown on a map does not mean they *must* be. Whereas maps are excellent for presenting the spatial relations between places, other kinds of visualizations can better show how geographical information appears within a text and how place references relate to literary elements such as characters. This section will explore non-cartographical ways of representing geographical relations within literary texts, using examples from Balzac, but in ways that can be used to explore any literary text.[6] The primary tools will be bubblelines, line graphs, and network graphs. Certainly, other types of diagrams like bar graphs, timelines, and pie charts can perform similar functions, complementing maps in representing geographical information.[7] These types of diagrams can display analytics and be used in conjunction with maps or network graphs. If the audience of the visualization is sufficiently familiar with the locations of the places discussed, other diagrams, such as bar graphs and network graphs, can be more enlightening as they reveal different aspects of geographical information other than location.

2.5.1 Bubblelines and Line Graphs

Line and bar graphs can represent frequencies, such as the number of times a place is mentioned within a specific slice of text, or they can represent quantities, such as the number of characters associated with a place. In the case of bar graphs, they reveal quantitative information and relationships between numbers more precisely than a map and more visually intuitively than a table. Stacked bar graphs can reveal, for example, the proportion of place references in each novel or series of novels to a specific place, region, or country. Similarly, a flow diagram can show the proportion of regional place references in each novel and series. Often numbers are best presented in a table, however, and bar or line graphs are better for presenting changes in numbers or frequencies over time. These types of graphs are ideal for visualizing literary texts because page, chapter, or volume numbers can be used to show how

---

[6] Diagrams combine text and image into a visual form of communication that is distinct from math, text, and images (Bender and Marrinan, 2010). Different diagram types emphasize distinct aspects of the data and are appropriate for only some purposes (maps emphasize geographical information; network graphs emphasize relationality, etc.).

[7] Tableau is a powerful suite of tools for presenting geographical information using visualizations that combine maps and analytical charts like line and bar graphs.

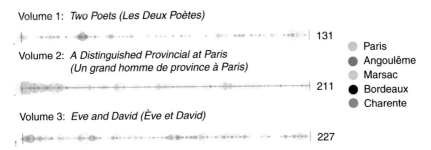

Volume 1: *Two Poets (Les Deux Poètes)*

131

Volume 2: *A Distinguished Provincial at Paris*
          (Un grand homme de province à Paris)

211

Volume 3: *Eve and David (Ève et David)*

227

- Paris
- Angoulême
- Marsac
- Bordeaux
- Charente

Figure 8 Most-referenced places within France in Balzac's *Lost Illusions*

various features appear and disappear within the text. Pie charts and other diagrams can represent proportions – for example, the number of times a place is referenced as a fraction of the total of all place references in a text or of all words in a text – but are less helpful in presenting temporal information.

One of the most "literary" elements of literary geographies is the placement of place references within the text and how readers perceive these place references. Are they settings? Part of an analogy? Or are they related to character traits such as nationality or occupation? Along with close reading and other techniques to assess the role of toponyms within a literary text, we can use bubblelines and other visualization techniques to get an idea of how these place references appear in a text from a macro perspective, otherwise known as distant reading. Since *The Human Comedy* contains multiple narrative series and not merely subplots, the narrative structure contains several discrete series that cannot be said to constitute one plot or be understood as part of one novel. For that reason, I will compare and analyze the place references of *Lost Illusions*, a series of three novels that form one *Bildungsroman* that takes place in the provinces, then in Paris, and then in the provinces again. *Lost Illusions* is the story of Lucien de Rubempré and his arrival in Paris, then his departure back to Angoulême and, eventually, the small town of Marsac in the same region. Figure 8 shows the textual order of the most commonly referenced places in *Lost Illusions*.[8]

We can see in Figure 8 that Paris is the place that is explicitly referenced the most in all three books of *Lost Illusions*. This is not a surprising finding for *Un grand homme de province à Paris* (volume 2), which is set in Paris and explores the misadventures of Lucien as he carves out a role for himself in the society of

---

[8] "Paris" includes adjectives like "parisien," nouns like "Parisienne," and other variants of the word "Paris." Angoulême includes derivative adjectives and nouns, as well as the former region of "Angoumois," of which Angoulême was the capital and main population center. England or English tokens include "Angelerre," "anglais(e)(s)," "Anglais(e)(s)," etc. *Lost Illusions* does not contain variants for the other toponyms in this list like "Marsac" and "Venise."

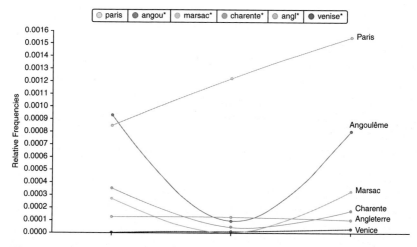

Figure 9 Line graph of the frequency of sample mentioned places in Balzac's *Lost Illusions* (3 vols.)

the capital, but the frequency of references to Paris in the other volumes is less predictable. On a bubbleline visualization, the size of the bubbles indicates the number of times the token occurs in that segment of the text. Bubblelines can visually present occurrences of a small number of word strings in various parts of a text. Since the bubbles can overlap, there is a limit to the number of colors that can be easily perceived, but approximately ten strings can appear in the same bubbleline and be visually distinguished. In this visualization, we can see that Bordeaux appears in small numbers somewhat regularly, whereas Marsac and Charente appear more sporadically but in higher numbers.

Figure 9 shows similar data plotted on a line graph of relative frequencies. Here we see that Paris is easily the most frequently mentioned place across the series and that Angoulême and Marsac dip significantly in the second volume. The underlying data visualized here are a count of the number of times each token or word appears as a proportion of the total words in that part of the text. Frequencies for toponyms are much lower than the most common words like determiners (i.e., "un[e]," "le," "la," etc.) or prepositions (i.e., "à," "de," etc.). Toponyms will rarely rival these words that form a part of basic French grammar.

Comparing occurrences of "England" and related adjectives ("Angelerre," "anglais[e][s]," "Anglais[e][s]," etc.) to Venice ("Venise"), two of the foreign places mentioned the most in this trilogy, we see that foreign cities like Venice barely register in any of the three books in terms of frequency, especially compared to Paris or England (Figure 9). This is not true of all Balzac texts, notably texts set in a foreign location like *Séraphîta* and *Adieu*, but in *Lost Illusions*, the foreign place references are far outnumbered by references to the most common French places. There are 89 total references to foreign places in *Lost Illusions*, including to Tangiers, Constantinople, Westphalia, Stockholm, and other places rarely mentioned in *The Human Comedy*. Most of these places are only mentioned once, with the duchy of Courtland (Lithuania), Beijing (China), Valencia (Spain), and Barcelona (Spain) the only precise locations mentioned more than once. Altogether, places in Spain are mentioned 12 times, and places in Great Britain and Italy are mentioned 8 times each. Any particular foreign place will be mentioned many fewer times than Paris, Angoulême, Marsac, or Charente. Mentions of country names and nationalities may approach the frequency of a place like Angoulême but will still be nowhere near as frequent as references to Paris. These bubblelines and line graphs show that references to places in *Lost Illusions* are correlated with the setting, and those place references that are not settings appear with a low but consistent frequency.

2.5.2 Place and Character Networks

Network graphs are useful for showing relations between places or between places and other features of fiction like characters or chapters because they emphasize connections rather than locations. They are less helpful than maps in presenting latitudes and longitudes of unfamiliar places. Network graphs can also display hidden connections or a lack of connection in a visually intuitive way. Network graphs can be convenient for exploring the relationship between characters and places, especially intertextually or in large corpora that a reader might have trouble analyzing without such a reading aid.

Figure 10 is a network graph of places in Asia, the Middle East, and the Orient in *The Human Comedy* connected to the characters associated with each place. This network is known as a bipartite graph because it connects nodes of two types: characters and places. The nodes, or circles, are sized according to the number of times the place or character is mentioned. We can immediately see that the largest circles represent the geographically largest places and vaguest terms, which occur more frequently in the text: the "Orient," Asia ("l'Asie"), India ("l'Inde"). The edges, or lines connecting the circles, indicate travel to those places but also analogies in which a character is compared to that place, as well as other associations that do not involve physical travel.

The character with the highest number of associations to places in Asia is Charles Mignon; thus, the node representing him is by far the largest of any character (Figure 10). Mignon is associated with Siberia, China, Malaysia, Asia Minor, Canton, the South China Sea, Java, and Malaysia. The places span Balzac's Asia from Siberia to Java. (Japan and Korea, as well as regions and cities in those countries, are strangely absent in *The Human Comedy*, perhaps

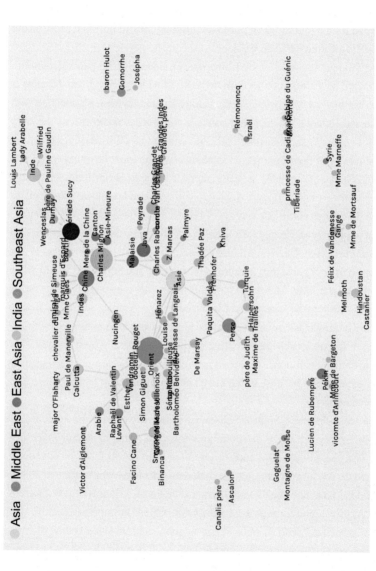

Figure 10 Network graph of places in Asia, the Middle East, and the Orient linked to associated characters in Balzac's *The Human Comedy*

due to the absence of European colonies there. Japan is mentioned rarely and Korea does not appear.) For Balzac, China was one of the few centers of civilization that rivaled Europe in its achievements and longevity (Bui and Le Huenon, 2017). He associates China with merchants like Mignon, as well as writing, porcelain, the performing arts, and Chinese court dress.[9] Whereas India and Southest Asia mostly appear as locations for trading posts and mines, China is referenced for a wider range of purposes, although it still does not serve as the primary setting for any Balzac stories.

Beyond Mignon's connections to China, we can also see in this network diagram that he does not have direct connections to the Middle East or the Orient. Mignon is connected indirectly to the Orient via the banker Nucingen, who is associated with China and the Orient. The fact that bankers and traders are some of the only characters to connect the two main hubs of Asia in this network diagram is yet another reminder of their importance in connecting the most far-flung regions of the world. Balzac references a large number of places in India (Calcutta, Pondicherry, the Ganges, diamond mines in the "Grandes Indes"), as well as using an antiquated name for India, "Hindoustan." These places in India are connected with a broad range of characters and not to one character making a grand journey like Charles Mignon. Since many of the references to the "Indes" are part of a backstory and not very detailed, it can be hard to tell when Balzac means the East Indies (Asia) and when he means the West Indies (Americas). Further, the characters connected to the Antilles are often tied to Pondicherry or Hindustan, revealing that the East and West Indies are more closely connected in the imaginary than their geographical distance would suggest. The Indian subcontinent is fragmented in this network graph, appearing in various parts of the diagram, in part because of the large number of different terms Balzac uses for the same region.

We can see in Figure 10 that the character-place network for the Middle East and the Orient is even more discontinuous than the Asian character-place network. In fact, the Middle East and the Orient are not consistently linked to one another and do not form communities or subnetworks in a technical sense. Places in the Middle East like the Levant, Persia ("la Perse"), Palmyra ("Palmyre"), Arabia ("Arabie"), and Smyrna are linked to the Orient through association with characters associated with it; only Persia is connected to places other than the Orient. The combination of the centrality of the Orient in the place-character network and the number of references to it shows the importance of the concept in

---

[9] The literature on Balzac and the Orient and on Balzac and China is voluminous. For a sense of recent approaches to Balzac and China, as well as the reception of Balzac's works in China by Maoists and contemporary readers, see *Balzac et la Chine. La Chine et Balzac* (Bui and Le Huenen, 2017).

Balzac's conception of Asia and the Middle East. The high number of references to China but the small number of connections to the Orient in relation to its frequency shows that Balzac conceptualizes the Orient as vaguely Middle Eastern. However, there are exceptions. Places like Israel ("Israel"), Syria ("la Syrie"), and Mount Sinai ("la Montagne de Moises") are only connected to one other character each, none of whom are connected to other places; for this reason, they are not connected to the main component of the network and are less central to Balzac's network of associations with the Orient.

One of the most valuable aspects of network graphs is showing the structure of relations as a whole. For example, the places that link China with Asia include Malaysia, Calcutta, and Java. This is not a strong set of associations because of the small number of edges or connections, but it does show that Maritime South Asia is perceived as an intermediary region tied to the concept of Asia and to China through figures like Charles Mignon, and not directly to the Orient. Persia and Turkey ("la Turquie") play a similar role in connecting Asia with the Orient and are less connected to China and India. There is, therefore, some influence of geographical proximity in the structure of the network, but the primary logic is the opposition between Asia and the Orient; other places are mostly either unconnected to the primary element or serve as intermediaries to these prominent places. Many of the places associated with only one character or two characters who are not associated with other places in Asia are in the Middle East. Places like Israel, Gomora, and Syria appear very infrequently in *The Human Comedy* and are associated with only one or two characters. Beijing is associated with three characters, but none of those characters are associated with other places in Asia or the Middle East.

Despite the cliché of the feminized Orient, for Balzac, fewer female characters than male characters are associated with the Orient or Asia. Female characters associated with Asia or China include Paquita Valdès, Duchesse de Langeais, and Mme Claes. The Duchesse de Langeais is also associated with the Orient, as are Séraphîta and Esther. These female characters are indeed often stereotyped as "exotic" and do not travel to the locations to which they are compared in often sexist ways. The female characters associated with Asia and the Orient are less central to the network than the male characters.

Balzac's Asia is the Asia of European colonization, including French, Dutch, and British colonies. He does not have much interest in places like Korea, the Philippines, and Japan that were not colonized by European powers in his lifetime or that were colonized by the Spanish. The characters most associated with Asia are traders and slave traders who exploit Asian peoples. Similarly, the characters most associated with the West Indies are investors in mining and other exploitative projects (Charles Mignon, Gobseck, etc.). The network diagram makes evident how much traders connect France and Paris to places in Asia and the Middle East that otherwise have very little representation in Balzac's work.

2.6 In the Shadow of the Empire

The most far-flung and culturally diverse places in *The Human Comedy* tend to be associated with male figures, generally the fathers and grandfathers of the series' main characters. The most cosmopolitan characters illustrate this tendency to associate worldliness with masculinity, age, and adventure (Table 6).

Table 6 Characters with most foreign associations in *The Human Comedy*

Character (Occupation)	References	Distinct associated places	Top associated places (Outside of France)
Colonel Chabert (Military Officer)	18	15	Germany (5), Lithuania (5), Americas, Austria, Egypt, Italy, Poland, Russia, Sainte-Hélène
Charles Mignon (Trader)	18	11	China (5), Germany (2), Malaysia (2), Russia (2), Belgium, Italy, India, Java, Turkey
Baron Hulot (Military Officer)	17	15	Germany (3), Algeria (2), Spain (2), Italy (2), Poland (2), Belgium, Belorussia, Palestine
Général de Montriveau (Military Officer)	14	11	Belgium, Egypt, Italy, Belorussia, Poland, Senegal, Russia
Charles Grandet (Merchant, Trader)	11	11	Germany (2), United States, Great Britain, Java, Portugal, Saint-Thomas
Gobseck (Merchant, Trader)	11	10	Argentina, Belgium, Haiti, India, Portugal, Saint-Thomas
Z. Marcas	10	10	Russia (2), Germany, Austria, Great Britain, Malaysia, Syria, Turkey

Charles Mignon, the father of Modeste Mignon, marries Bettina Wallenrod in Frankfurt; before his marriage, he traveled from the Antilles to Asia, trafficking in opium and indigo, among other goods. Most chillingly, he trades in slaves. Trade brings Mignon to Java and Malaysia; he goes to India six times. Mignon is jailed in Siberia with Dumay, and he ends up in Constantinople penniless. Compare this exotic and unlikely resumé with the life of his daughter Modeste. She does not travel; the only foreign place with which she is associated is her mother's native Germany, of which she is said to be an incarnation. This is her only connection to the world outside of France. The contrast between Modeste Mignon and her father is an extreme case, but it shows how gendered travel is in *The Human Comedy*. Experience of the world is associated with previous generations of French men, not the relatively sedentary men of the July Monarchy or their wives and daughters.

Other characters who rival Charles Mignon in terms of the number and diversity of places they have traveled include the Napoleonic officers such as Colonel Chabert and the Général de Montriveau. The dashing lover of the Duchesse de Langeais, Armand de Montriveau has been deployed in nearly every major French theater of war of the period. Handsome, charming, and intelligent, he is the closest *The Human Comedy* comes to a Romantic hero. A participant in campaigns to Europe and to North and West Africa, Montriveau even takes a scholarly interest in Africa, traveling to the countries in central Africa and learning native African languages. Montriveau takes part in the 1808 attack on Capri, Italy, and later explores upper Egypt; in 1815, he is taken captive at Waterloo. He seduces the Duchesse de Langeais in Spain with his tales of battle and voyages in the Orient. Like Charles Mignon, the Général de Montriveau lives an adventurous life. Because of his military vocation, he travels to the ends of the earth and returns to Europe. His lover, the Duchesse de Langeais, is more limited in her movements, though she does travel from France to Spain and then to the convent on a Mediterranean island where she becomes an abbess. Colonel Chabert is one of the most cosmopolitan characters and one of the rare protagonists to be associated with many foreign places; he is also one of the oldest protagonists, representative of the Empire rather than the Monarchy of July. It is said that he has traveled most of the world with Boutin; he took part in the battle of Iena, commanded a regiment of the French cavalry at Eylau, and was committed to a mental hospital in Stuttgart. These well-traveled military officers do not make all of their journeys for military reasons, but it is hard to imagine they would have traveled to such a large number of far-off places if they had a different vocation. Even when the characters never occur in the same novel or scene, they often have experience fighting in the same battles or know someone who has experience fighting in a battle that marks both historical time and a shared experience of the world outside of France.

The links between the French Empire and Balzac's map of the world also explain the comparative lack of focus on the Americas. Even though it is not made clear where else he has been, it is said that "America is one of the rare places that Chabert and Boutin haven't been" (*Colonel Chabert*) – that is, even the most well-traveled characters have rarely made it to the Americas. *The Black Sheep* [*La Raboullieuse*] has the most references to the Americas because of a character's trip to the New World. Charles Grandet, a cousin and suitor of Eugénie Grandet of the titular novel, is one of the few characters to travel there. He goes to the Americas as a slave trader, a business that takes him from Africa to the New World and then on to China. We can see in Charles Grandet the pessimistic view Balzac has of capitalism and of trading. Other cosmopolitan merchants like Gobseck show both Balzac's negative view of capitalism and his anti-Semitism. Gobseck is associated with a different set of foreign countries (Argentina, Belgium, Haiti, India, Portugal, and Saint-Thomas), but he, like Grandet, brings together countries from the Old World and the New World, from Asia and the Americas.

Unlike Grandet, Gobseck is stereotyped as a Jewish miser whose art collection is unearned and unappreciated; if anything, Balzac is kinder to the slave-trading Grandet. Many backstories in the Americas and Asia are connected to exploitation. Gobseck is paradigmatic in this sense, creating ingenious but morally suspect enterprises in other countries, mainly former French colonies. In the newly recognized Republic of Haiti, formerly Saint-Domingue, Gobseck has himself appointed a member of a commission to liquidate the holdings of French colonists and their heirs. He then invents a firm using the name of two of his associates (Werbrust and Gigonnet) who have put up the money to found the business (*CH*, vol. VI, p. 419). This business buys up the claims, properties, and possessions of the desperate or those wanting to sell immediately to avoid future risks. At the same time, he makes deals under his own name with the large landowners who are less desperate to sell and accepts what Balzac refers to as "gifts" for his services, including snuff boxes and candle books. By trading under his colleagues' names as well as his own, Gobseck is able to buy up a large number of possessions devalued by the transition from a colony to an independent republic. At the same time, while distributing the payments exacted by the French government from the new Haitian Republic, he surreptitiously enriches himself. This form of exploitation is intimately tied up with colonialism and capitalism. It is impossible to conceive of such an arrangement in a world where France was not a former colonial power with immense financial and military advantages over the young republic of Haiti. At the same time, the Jewishness of this particular character cannot be ignored in the narrator's claims that Gosbeck is a "usurer" who operates unscrupulously and takes everything without offering anything in return, a common claim of anti-Semites in the nineteenth century when Jewish people – rich and poor – were often unjustly blamed for the excesses of capitalism.

The Jewish miser and the worldly merchant-trader are independent tropes that Balzac brings together in the character of Gobseck, but they occur separately elsewhere (Table 6). The character of Charles Grandet has many of the same traits as Gobseck, without the sin of usury being attributed to his capitalist exploits. These merchant-trader characters venture even further than the soldier-officer types and follow less predictable patterns since their travels do not mirror historical events, as the movements of participants in the Napoleonic Wars do. They can be French or foreign-born but are characterized by connections to the Antilles, Asia, or Africa, places far less frequently referenced in *The Human Comedy* than are cities and battle sites in Italy, Germany, or Russia. These far-off places, from Asia to the Americas, connect risk-taking characters like adventurers and merchants, well beyond the confines of Paris. Unlike Italy, Spain, Russia, or Norway, these locations never serve as the primary setting for a story but always occupy the backstory. Whereas Napoleonic battles are experienced and remembered by at least some of the characters, and even by protagonists like Colonel Chabert, stories of ill-gotten gains in the East or West Indies are usually related only in order to show the character of the person benefiting from the arrangement and rarely to create sympathy for the exploited. Even in *Adieu*, a rare depiction of battle and its effects that delves into themes of madness and healing in the face of inhuman cruelty, most of the characters are French and the impacts of war and colonialism are mainly seen in terms of their effect on the French invaders, rather than the Russian defenders (Cnockaert, 2009). While the French traders and soldiers are coded as exploitative, most of the plots point toward exploitation of other French people or Parisians, rather than Indigenous or local people. Balzac's fixation on colonial domination in the empire is part of a broader tendency of realist literature to maintain the power relations inherent in colonial relations within the fictional world (Baker, 2009, p. 5), at the same time as portraying foreign figures or travelers as potentially emancipatory by virtue of their cosmopolitanism and exoticism.

The characters associated with these diverse places are a small proportion of the total characters in *The Human Comedy*. By comparing the social networks of characters to the places with which they are associated, we can see the overwhelming importance of military and commercial networks in the exotic backstories of characters and in connecting the world of Paris to the broader world. Balzac's *The Human Comedy* is the first fictional global network that negotiates what it means to live in a global world: to theoretically be able to travel anywhere, even if one never does; to know people, or to know of people, who have traveled almost everywhere; to live in a country that has invaded countries throughout the world; to be subject to the whims of global capitalists and shifting markets. Although most of Balzac's characters never leave France, they are aware of the diverse cultures and practices of other civilizations, and they feel themselves to be living in a global age. Through his innovation of recurring characters, Balzac conjures a global network of human relationships that has few precedents in world literature. Balzac's *société* of more than two thousand characters is a feat rarely repeated, and that makes possible the truly global reach of *The Human Comedy*.

Balzac's literary geography is built on distinctions between (1) the primary settings in Paris and a few provincial locations, often fictionalized, (2) side plots and backstories that range far more widely but remain predominantly European, and (3) place references within the narration that range worldwide but do not mark the actual setting of the novel, tending instead to be symbolic, analogical, or learned references that establish a broader narrative horizon of place-making. The traders and soldiers who dominate the backstory and who connect the most far-flung places are, in some ways, analogous to the ambitious young provincial men who seek to dominate the French capital. Like their fathers and grand-fathers before them, these young men face immense risks and potential losses; the primary difference is that they act on a national rather than a global stage, and success on this national stage is presented as even more vital than conquering the globe.

3 Proust's Imagined Map

3.1 Proust's Reimagined Places

The literary geography of Marcel Proust's *In Search of Lost Time* is a case study for fiction that draws upon historical places but also distances itself from historical references. It is necessary to consider nonlinear time (Kristeva, 1994) and the rhetorical force of the narrator in shaping the relation between place, time, and character in Proust's work (Dupuy, 2019). Despite the fictional status of two of the primary settings, Combray and Balbec, the geography of Proust's magnum opus is coextensive with the French human geography of the time at a deeper level than surface references, including cultural and socioeconomic differences between regions and parts of regions. His evocation of the Guermantes way and its association with the wealthiest and most noble elements of Combray's society is grounded in both French socioeconomics and regional history. Proust's literary geography, then, stands in contrast to Balzac's realist geography, without entirely breaking from French cultural geography.

Proust's literary geography is distant from historical cartography but not entirely independent of history. The geography of *In Search of Lost Time* has been studied almost as frequently as Balzac's geography from a thematic perspective. Places in Proust have been mapped many times, starting with André Ferré's dissertation in 1936, completed not long after the last volume of Proust's *roman fleuve* was published. Ferré, in many ways, set the tone for academic discussions of Proust's geography. He denied that the main settings of Proust's novel, notably the fictional towns of Combray and Balbec, were the equivalents of the historical towns on which they were based; nevertheless, he used elements of those historical cities' layouts to produce maps of their fictional counterparts (Ferré, 1939). While academics have generally been skeptical of the historicity and geographical realism of Proust's settings, tourists and the French government have embraced the sites of Proust's childhood as illustrations of the reality of his fiction, going so far as to rename the city of Illiers, which Proust had rebaptized "Combray," as Illiers-Combray, a nod to its historical past and to Proust's more famous reimagining of the small French city. Despite the differences between Combray and Illiers, we can geolocate Combray near Illiers based on descriptions of the town. The same goes for Balbec and the real town that inspires it, Cabourg. Many of the other locations in *In Search of Lost Time* are historical or said to be near Balbec or Combray. Figure 11 shows the place references in or near France in *In Search of Lost Time*. The circles are sized according to the number of references to each place in all six volumes of the novel; the historical and nonhistorical places are indicated.[10]

For the most part, in Proust, places outside of France, even those very near to France, use their historical toponyms. The many cities in Italy mentioned, as well as cities in the Netherlands, Belgium, Germany, and England, are referenced by name. The fictional places in *In Search of Lost Time* are disproportionately near Combray and Balbec. Most of the fictional places in *In Search of Lost Time* are located in Normandy: of the 57 total fictional places (mentioned 477 times), 41 places (mentioned 286 times) are in that region. Fictional places in Normandy range from absolutely central to the fictional world, such as Balbec, mentioned 96 times, to minor, such as the forest of Chantepie, mentioned 5 times, and Bagatelle, the farm restaurant near Balbec that is mentioned only twice. Many of these places are either very near Balbec, along the local railway line, or along the seashore. They are almost all places to which the narrator travels rather than hearing or speaking about them. Some of the fictional places outside of Normandy include princely seats like the Château

---

[10] *The Prisoner* and *The Fugitive* are sometimes treated as separate volumes and at other times combined into one volume, in part to account for the fact that they are much shorter than the other volumes; thus some editions count a total of six volumes while others count seven.

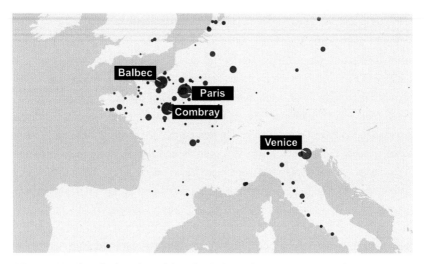

Figure 11 Historical and nonhistorical places in or near France in Proust's *In Search of Lost Time*

de Charlus, located near the center of Burgundy, and Voisenon, the Prince de Guermantes's château near Paris. The most prominent and frequently cited fictional place other than Combray and Balbec is Guermantes, the country home of the Guermantes family near Combray and the end point of the Guermantes way, the path by Combray that eventually leads to the home of the preeminent noble family in the novel.

3.2 A Model of Post-realist Geography

For the sake of this analysis, I am referring to fictions like *In Search of Lost Time* as "post-realist" if they come after the realist nineteenth-century articulation of literary geography and, in some ways, undercut or play with the correspondence of literary places with points on the globe. In Marc Brousseau's terminology, post-realist novels are "roman-géographes" that chart their own geographies in the text itself (Brousseau, 1996). Unlike "non-realist" or "anti-realist" fictions, these literary geographies do relate to historical geographies but not in the mostly direct way. Many of the fictions that create a post-realist geography are modernist or postmodernist, and they may intentionally undercut the claims to historicity of realist fiction; that said, some of the principles for analyzing and visualizing post-realist literary geography may be relevant to fictions that create semi-realistic geographies, such as ones that predate realist geographies or that are related in a complex way to historical geographies, even if they are not technically post-realist, such as Nerval's poetic geographies, which are nearly contemporaneous with

Balzac's (Chambers, 1969). In Proust's case, in *In Search of Lost Time,* he combines historical settings like Venice and Paris with invented or reimagined settings like Combray, the town where the narrator spent his first years and also where the narration of the *roman fleuve* begins. However, the fictional settings of Proust's novel are not limited to Combray and Balbec, the seaside town mentioned even more frequently than Combray. Instead, most of the provincial settings of *In Search of Lost Time*, including the smaller towns around Combray and Balbec, are fictional or fictionalized versions of historical places. This fictionalization puts a barrier between the fictional world of *In Search of Lost Time* and our historical understanding of France such that we cannot fill in the gaps with whatever knowledge we have of French geography. At the same time, places like Combray and Balbec are explicitly located in particular regions at specific historical times.

While Proust refers to many of the same places Balzac does, notably Paris, other European capitals, and some French regions, there are not nearly as many place references in Proust as in Balzac; this lower number of place references is in part a function of fewer volumes and shorter texts; it is also a function of a smaller number of distinct places appearing. And yet the overall proportion of explicit place references to Paris, the provinces, and the rest of the world is similar in Proust and Balzac despite the vast differences in scale (Table 7). The smaller number of distinct places referenced in Proust allows him to return to the same places and bring new associations to them, but it reduces the encyclopedic quality of his geography.

We see the same tripartite classification of places between (1) those in Paris, which are the most specific and tied to historical places, even if they are fictional, such as a fictional house on a historical street or "near" a historical monument; (2) those in the provinces, which can be quite specific but are more often fictional; and (3) the rest of the world, where places are overwhelmingly vague but historical. In terms of place references outside of France, Proust is even more conventional than Balzac, sticking to cities like Venice, Madrid, Moscow, and New York, rather than vaguer place references like the Orient, the Indies, or the Americas. Proust does reference places in the Middle East, primarily in biblical references, but otherwise shows far less interest in anthropological or sociological comparisons to contemporary societies and peoples outside of France. Like Balzac, Proust references a wide variety of places in France, especially in passing, though not nearly the same number as Balzac. Indeed, Proust has even less interest in eastern, southern, or southwestern France or the Alps. Likewise, we see less interest in Eastern Europe, the Baltics, and Russia than in Balzac. This reflects Proust's lesser interest in battlefield narratives but not in war, as World War I is a central

Table 7 Place references by region in Proust's *In Search of Lost Time*

Region	References to region	Distinct places referenced within region	Volumes with references	Top volume
Paris / Île de France	141	16	6	*The Prisoner / The Fugitive*
Provinces	602	81	6	*Sodom and Gomorrah*
World (Outside France)	186	42	6	*The Guermantes Way*
Total	929	153	6	*Sodom and Gomorrah*

Table 8 Most-referenced countries in Proust's *In Search of Lost Time*

Country or region	References to country	Distinct places referenced in country	Volumes with references	Top volume
Italy	94	15	6	*The Prisoner / The Fugitive*
Netherlands / Belgium	34	7	5	*The Guermantes Way*
Germany	18	4	6	*Sodom and Gomorrah*
England	9	2	5	*Within a Budding Grove*
Morocco	6	2	1	*The Guermantes Way*
World Total	186	42	6	*The Guermantes Way*

concern of the final volume, especially its impact on Paris and northern France.

The most-referenced places outside of France in *In Search of Lost Time* are in Italy, the Netherlands and Belgium, Germany, England, and Morocco (Table 8).

Proust is strongly focused on regions closest to France and only makes occasional references to places that are much further off. Foreign places Proust references are primarily located on the English Channel ("La Manche") and in the Mediterranean basin (France, Italy), and, to a lesser extent, the rest of Europe. The book that features the most international place references overall is *The Guermantes Way,* but all volumes contain references to places outside of France. The dispersion of foreign places across volumes shows no apparent pattern, aside from *The Prisoner / The Fugitive,* in which the narrator travels to Italy. Proust's geography is even more Eurocentric than Balzac's. The only truly far-off places he mentions are Russia, Susa, Egypt, Florida, and New York. For the most part, his foreign place references are centered on the Mediterranean, with Morocco and especially places in Italy receiving large numbers of mentions. He names Venice, to which the narrator travels, by far the most number of times (40), but most major Italian cities are mentioned several times, including Rome (4). Regions like Parma (7) and Sicily (3) also appear, as well as ancient locations like Pompeii (4). At the country or regional level, there is a huge gap between Italy (94), which is mentioned by far the most, and the next most-referenced region of the Netherlands and Belgium (34) and then other European countries like Germany (18) or England (9). Not only are there more distinct places mentioned in Italy (15) but the average number of times that a place is mentioned is higher. The average number of times a place in Italy is mentioned is 6, versus 5 for the Netherlands and Belgium and 4.5 for Germany.

As with Balzac, Paris is the most-referenced city both in the world and in France, and the next most-cited cities are also in France. Much of the debate about Proust's geography has focused on the status of fictional locations, notably Combray and Balbec. Some of these debates have overstated the "positivistic" geographical orientation of realist literature and understated the geographical realism of post-realist literature like *In Search Lost Time.* There is little doubt that Combray and Balbec cannot be decisively geolocated and that any attribution of a precise latitude and longitude to Proust's fictional places is necessarily approximate. At the same time, provincial place references in Proust obey many of the rules of provincial place references in realist fiction: they mix historical and ahistorical places, focus on the experiences of the characters, identify archetypical buildings like churches and landmarks like rivers, and ascribe broad class significations to places in a manner that recalls Balzac. Indeed, many of the places in Proust's provincial scenes are archetypical of the French provinces (the cathedral, the train stop, the farm-restaurant) and are not so much ahistorical as idealized or romanticized versions of historical places. Other locations mentioned frequently are idyllic locations associated either with royalty (Fontainebleau) or fictional

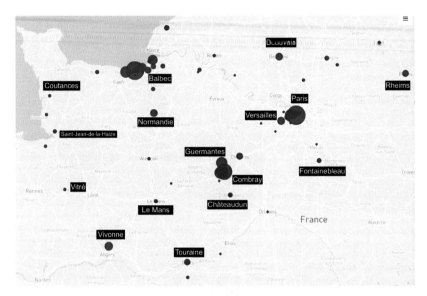

Figure 12 Map of place references in Proust's *In Search of Lost Time*, detail,
Paris-Combray-Normandy

nobles in the book (Guermantes) that exist in a more literary sphere that recalls earlier literary motifs more than realist ones (Figure 12).

One perfect example of the issues with literary cartography in post-realist fiction is Combray itself. Already in 1939, André Ferré, the geographer and Proust critic, had established that places in Proust echoed historical places and places known to Proust in his lifetime, but that many of these places, especially in the provinces, did not correspond to historical maps in an unproblematic way (Ferré, 1939). For example, Combray has many aspects in common with Illiers, a town where Proust spent a good deal of time as a young man, but Proust made the very intentional choice to use a fictional name and only some aspects of the town in his writing.

Ferré cleverly created a hand-drawn map of Combray retaining only those elements that appear in *In Search of Lost Time*: the pavilion, the church, the grand avenue, the old church, the Loire, the cemetery, the road to Chartres, etc. This low-tech solution allowed him to customize what appears and even the density and placement of buildings, bodies of water, and roads that might not fit the literary geography precisely. I have redrawn this map digitally with the elements of Illiers retained in Combray labeled, including the garden belonging to Proust's relatives that now bears his name and his aunt's house, which is now a museum dedicated to the writer (Figure 13).

Many of the most-referenced places in Proust are fictional (Table 9). Of course, there are Balbec (96) and Combray (74), mentioned less frequently

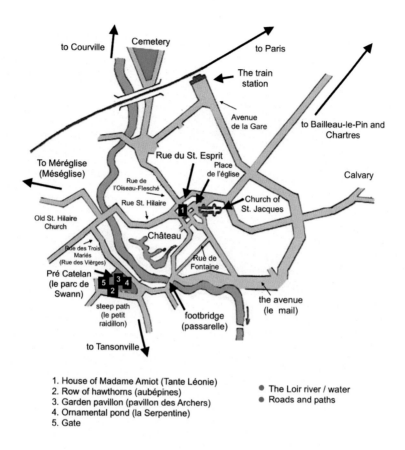

Figure 13 Map of Proust's Combray, based on Ferré's map "Plan d'Illiers avec les éléments retenus dans Combray"

than Paris (111) but more than Venice (40). Many other frequently referenced places are fictional or fictionalized. Most of them are also either located in Normandy or in or near the Loire Valley. The most-referenced places appear in all six volumes. Places that appear in fewer volumes are also referenced fewer times. We see, then, the structural effect of returning to the same places again and again in the narration, where the most significant places recur throughout the text, and even less significant places are mentioned in multiple volumes. Instead of seeing a strong association between individual places and individual volumes, even places that are mentioned few times recur across volumes and are mentioned by multiple characters, who often do not know each other and are not aware of what others have said about the place.

Table 9 Most-referenced cities and towns in Proust's *In Search of Lost Time*

City or town	Region	Fictional or historical	References to city or town	Number of books with references	Top book
Paris	Île de France	Historical	111	6	*The Prisoner / The Fugitive*
Balbec	Normandie	Fictional	96	6	*Within a Budding Grove*
Combray	Centre-Val de Loire	Fictional	74	6	*Swann's Way*
Venice	Italy	Historical	40	6	*The Prisoner / The Fugitive*
Doncières	Normandie	Fictional	34	6	*The Guermantes Way*
Méséglise-La-Vineuse	Centre-Val de Loire	Fictional	24	6	*Swann's Way*
Guermantes	Centre-Val de Loire	Fictional	23	6	*The Guermantes Way*
Rivebelle	Normandie	Fictional	22	5	*Sodom and Gomorrah*
La Raspelière	Normandie	Fictional	17	3	*Sodom and Gomorrah*
Roussain-Le-Lin	Normandie	Fictional	15	3	*Swann's Way*
Incarville	Normandie	Fictional	14	3	*Sodom and Gomorrah*
Tansonville	Centre-Val de Loire	Fictional	14	4	*Swann's Way*
Total			929	6	

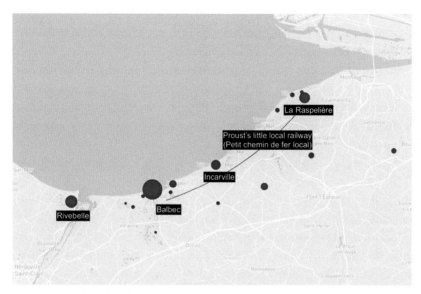

Figure 14 Proust's Balbec and the potential location of the little local railway

Thus, despite the lack of an exact correspondence of a place like Balbec or Rivebelle with a historical location, we have every reason to believe these places really exist in the narrator's world, in the sense of being visible and comprehensible to others. We can see an example of this ruminative effect of returning to the same places, even minor ones, giving a sense of shared reality that nevertheless does not correspond to a historical one, in Proust's "petit chemin de fer local," the local railway depicted as running from Balbec to Douville and composed of entirely fictional places; references to this railway cut across multiple plots and subplots (Figure 14). The little local train extends from Balbec to Douville and ostensibly fills in much of the area between these two stops, but it cannot be mapped onto a historical map of France because so many of the locations are fictional.[11] Nevertheless, many details are given across multiple volumes that allow the reader to learn much about these stops. We can therefore learn a great deal about how the train lines figure in the narrative by considering which places play the largest roles, in which volumes they appear, and which characters interact with or discuss each stop. The following are the most mentioned of the at least 38 stops along Proust's little local railway in order from most to least referenced:

Doncières (34) – a garrison town not far from Balbec. Saint-Loup is on military service there; the narrator and Albertine meet at the train station;

---

[11] Ferré does provide a non-geographical diagram of the train stops for the local train near Balbec that shows the likely order of the stops and how the tracks could fit together (Ferré 1939, p. 119).

Charlus and Morel meet there. The narrator describes the Hôtel de Flandre, restaurants, the train station, meetings with friends, and walks through the town at length. Doncières appears in all six volumes.

Saint-Mars-le-Vieux (15) – a station near Balbec where Charlus rents a house, and Charlus and Morel meet. The narrator plans excursions with Mme de Villeparisis there and later drives there; the steeples of the church are described; Albertine speculates about the origin of the name. It appears in *Sodom and Gomorrah*.

Incarville (14) – a small city with a casino that Brichot confuses with Balbec; M. de Crécy's castle is perched above Incarville; the etymology of the name comes from the village of Wiscar; the cliff is described. It appears in *Within a Budding Grove*, *Sodom and Gomorrah*, and *The Prisoner / The Fugitive*.

Maineville (11) – the last stop before Balbec on the little local railway. Its cliffs are visible from the Grand Hôtel and it has a luxury brothel. This stop appears in *Within a Budding Grove* and *Sodom and Gomorrah*.

Douville (9) – a stop for Féterne and La Raspelière that appears in *Within a Budding Grove* and *Sodom and Gomorrah*.

Parville-la-Bingard (8) – Parville is visible from La Raspelière; the narrator drops Albertine there after outings; Parville has visible cliffs. The stop appears in *Sodom and Gomorrah*.

Harambouville (5) – one of the places where passengers descend to eat or take a stroll; Mme Verdurin plans an outing there, and the name is said to be derived from "Herimbald's town." Harambouville appears in *Sodom and Gomorrah*.

Marcouville-L'Orgueilleuse (5) – a small town with a restored church that Albertine and the narrator visit and that is just visible from Rivebelle. The town appears in *Within a Budding Grove*, *The Prisoner / The Fugitive*, and *Sodom and Gomorrah*.

Pont-à-Couleuvre (5) – a stop where the manager of the Grand Hôtel meets the narrator. M de Cambremer says he has never seen snakes there and Brichot gives its etymology. Pont-à-Couleuvre appears in *Within a Budding Grove* and *Sodom and Gomorrah*.

La Sogne (4) – a stop near Balbec where Albertine goes to the races. La Sogne is the Cambremers' station, and it appears in *Within a Budding Grove* and *Sodom and Gomorrah*.

Graincourt-Saint-Vast (4) – first station after Doncières on the local railway, where Cottard of Mme Verdurin's "petit clan" catches the train; Ski and Cottard nearly miss the train; this stop is mentioned in *Sodom and Gomorrah*.

Saint-Pierre-des-Ifs (3) – Charlus rents a house there, and the narrator sees the girl with a cigarette there. This stop appears in *Sodom and Gomorrah*.

Grattevast (2) – a stop in the opposite direction from Féterne that appears in *Sodom and Gomorrah*.

The various train stops, which are enumerated across multiple volumes, especially in *Within a Budding Grove* and *Sodom and Gomorrah*, give the impression of being linked; these stops, especially the one in Doncières, are developed through successive ruminations on memories tied to those places. Many of the towns mentioned, like other places in Proust's Normandy, cannot be localized and are not drawn from Normandy at all. Many of the names of towns near Balbec are drawn from the region around Illiers. As Ferré argued, localizing these places in relation to Balbec is difficult since Balbec itself can be localized in several different places depending on which directions or orientation within the text one relies upon (Ferré, 1939, p. 106). Indeed, the little railway line is not precisely localizable in part because there are no historical places that act as anchors for the fictional places. Thus, the list of stops, even when we can put them in order, does not help us place them on a map. Unlike in Balzac, where fictional locations, such as inherited land and country houses, are sometimes linked to historical towns or natural features like mountains or rivers, Proust's railway is unmoored from all but the vaguest geographical and historical references like the coastline or proximity to other fictional towns. Plenty of geographical references to other fictional places ("near Balbec," "the first stop after Balbec," etc.) allow us to place some of the toponyms in relation to each other or in relation to vague geological features like seaside cliffs or rivers, but not to precise locations.

The little local railway is not the only impossible train in Proust. The route of another of Proust's trains, the 13h22 or 1:22 p.m. train from Paris to Balbec, though passing through historical stations, is anything but realistic. Ferré's map of the area around Balbec (Figure 15) depicts minor and major historical train lines as dotted and solid lines that show the routes the 1:22 p.m. train would have taken to pass through the various stops on the line in the order described in the text. Immediately we see that the sequence of stops requires an entirely illogical and convoluted path. Balbec is the sixth of the eleven stops for the train in this region. Thus it might seem logical that Balbec would be located somewhere along the coast between Pontorson, the fifth stop, and Lannion, the seventh, but this is merely an inference drawn from a route that, in but one unlikely example, has the train head south from Coutances all the way to Questembert, passing Pontorson, before doubling back north to finally make its stop in Pontorson. We can also see in the map that the names of places in Normandy that inspired Proust's naming of locations around Balbec are

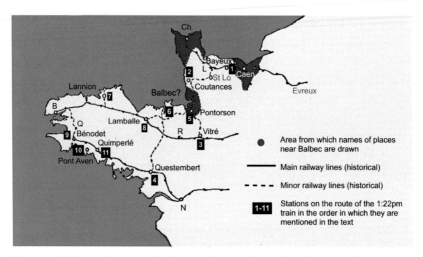

Figure 15 Map of Proust's Balbec and its environs, based on Ferré's map "Le pays de Balbec"

confined to three distinct regions that provide a vague indication of Balbec's location along the coast, but no precise position (Figure 15).

The ruminative nature of Proust's prose thus means that settings and place references are linked to one another associatively rather than tied to a setting that grounds the place references. The pseudo-historicity of the places along the train line is elevated by the fact that multiple characters take the train, refer to the railway, or otherwise interact with the railway, and some characters, notably Brisot and Albertine, talk about the origins and meanings of the names of the stops, even confusing one stop with another and correcting other characters. And yet the railway stops from Proust's trains are nearly impossible to align with historical stops on the existing train lines of the time in the order in which they are mentioned in the text. This sort of under-specified geography that can be experienced by different characters at various times and then discussed is more relational and less referential. It is because of this relational nature that rumination and return to the same places becomes heavy with significance rather than disorienting or troubling. Within the fictional world, Proust's geography makes sense, even if it is impressionistic; it is only when comparing against historical maps that the difficulties locating places and tracking the movements of characters become so evident.

Like Balzac, Proust mentions locations (historical or fictional) in the French provinces more than locations in Paris or the rest of the world. The provinces dominate without crowding out references to Paris or foreign places entirely in any one volume. The geographical distribution of places within the volumes of

Table 10 Regional place references by volume of Proust's *In Search of Lost Time*

Volume	Paris / Île de France	Provinces	World (outside France)	Total
Swann's Way	16% (30)	68% (129)	17% (32)	191
Within a Budding Grove	13% (19)	64% (98)	23% (35)	152
The Guermantes Way	15% (22)	54% (82)	31% (47)	151
Sodom and Gomorrah	7% (14)	84% (170)	9% (19)	203
The Prisoner / The Fugitive	23% (38)	51% (83)	25% (41)	162
Time Regained	26% (18)	57% (40)	17% (12)	70
Total	15% (141)	65% (602)	20% (186)	929

In Search of Lost Time is fairly consistent across volumes, despite the differences in length (Table 10).

Table 10 shows the proportion of place references in each volume for Paris, the provinces, and the rest of the world. Overall, the provinces constitute by far the highest proportion of references; as we have seen, many of these place references are fictional and are located primarily in reference to other fictional places. *Sodom and Gomorrah* contains more references to the provinces in general (84%), and to Normandy in particular, than it does to places in Paris (7%). The average proportion of place references to the provinces (65%) compared to Paris (15%) is already high, much higher than in Balzac. *Time Regained* has the highest proportion of references to Paris (26%), but a majority of place references are still to elsewhere in France (57%). Similarly, the proportion of place references outside of France ranges from 9% in *Sodom and Gomorrah* to 31% in *The Guermantes Way*, but references to foreign places are never the majority of references. That said, *Sodom and Gomorrah* has the largest number of place references overall and thus accounts for a large percentage of place references in all categories.

The predominance of fictional places in the provinces, especially in Normandy, grants a kind of otherworldly status to Balbec and its environs, and to Combray, with its Guermantes way and Swann's way as fictional orienting paths. These places are not anchored by specific references to historical places on the local level, but they are anchored referentially and relationally within a larger historical and geographical world that contains the lodestars of Paris, Venice, and other historic places. In many ways, we can better explore this ruminative, relational nature of place references in Proust by using visualizations like bubblelines and network graphs rather than maps, which form an essential starting point for places that can be localized approximately, but that cannot in isolation do justice to the complex forms of interrelation found between places and characters in a dense work like *In Search of Lost Time*. It is for this reason I have chosen Proust as an ideal literary geography to explore alternatives to maps in more detail.

3.3 Alternative Maps: Words, Characters, Place, and Time

In Search of Lost Time is a *Bildungsroman* that involves a young man who aspires to be both a socialite and a writer and who journeys from a small town to Paris, repeatedly and not in chronological order. As with *Lost Illusions* (see Figure 8), we can use bubbleline visualizations and line graphs to see how frequencies of toponyms change over different parts of Proust's text, and we can use network graphs to investigate associations between places and characters. We can make a one-to-one comparison between *In Search of Lost Time* and *Lost Illusions* in a way that would not be possible against the entire text of Balzac's *The Human Comedy*, yet it remains important to remember that Proust's time-line is not as simple as the one in *Lost Illusions.* The concept of timelines is hardly new in either Balzac or Proust studies. The question of the order in which events occur has been most debated by critics of *In Search of Lost Time*, due to gaps in the narration that make it difficult to determine when each event takes place. The timeline of *In Search of Lost Time* is much debated, and there have been multiple versions proposed (Genette, 1983; Landy, 2004). That said, the textual order of place references is not a subject of very much debate since the general order of the text has been established despite the fact that two volumes remained unfinished at Proust's death.

In Proust's narration, the way places and characters relate to one another is explicitly relational and associative, rather than deictic. Proust's narrator lays out the pattern of relations between place references and characters quite explicitly in a statement early in the section "Combray" of *Swann's Way*, the first volume in the novel.

> Je passais la plus grande partie de la nuit à me rappeler notre vie d'autrefois à Combray chez ma grand'tante, à Balbec, à Paris, à Doncières, à Venise, ailleurs encore, à me rappeler les lieux, les personnes que j'y avais connues, ce que j'avais vu d'elles, ce qu'on m'en avait raconté. (I: 18)

> I spent most of the night remembering our former life in Combray at my
> great-aunt's, in Balbec, Paris, Doncières, Venice, and elsewhere still, remem-
> bering the places, the people I had known there, what I had seen of them, what
> I had been told about them.

The narrator mixes remembered places and events with events told to
him in a way that makes it difficult to sort out experienced and remembered places from misremembered places or places evoked in relation to
events that never happened. The narrator makes repetitive references to
these core places – Combray, Balbec, Paris, Doncière – in an extended
rumination on the life he has lived in these various places, the people he
has met, events he has imagined or desired to happen, and things others
have told him about places, or even places others would like to go or
think others should go. The layers of counterfactual, hypothetical, remembered, and imagined places mingle with the settings of the events of his
life in a way that makes extracting stable geographical meanings suspect.
At the same time, many of the places he refers to (Combray, Balbec)
come back again and again. Other places that are significant for him
(Paris, Venice, The Hague) are historical places, and their historicity
matters in the text.

Figure 16 shows the occurrence of the terms "Combray," "Paris," and
"Balbec" in the seven-volume version of the text. On the right, the total number
of references to these terms is displayed.

Unsurprisingly, "Combray" is most frequent in the first third of *Swann's
Way*, a segment of the text entitled "Combray I," and recur throughout volume
1. The third part of that volume is entitled "Noms de pays: le nom," which
C. K. Scott Moncrieff translates as "Place-Names: The Name," stripping out
the regional concept of "pays." The opening of this section is a reflection on
places and the way literature represents them; it refers to all three primary
settings of the novel. "Combray" is far less frequent in volumes 2 to 6, except
for the beginning of volume 3 and the end of volume 6. "Combray" recurs
throughout much of *Time Regained* (volume 7), but not with the same frequency as in volume 1. Paris is frequently referenced throughout all seven
volumes, with the exception of parts of volumes 5 (*The Prisoner*) and 6 (*The
Fugitive*). Paris is most frequently referenced at the beginning of *Time
Regained* (volume 7) and fades throughout that volume. References to
"Balbec" are most frequent in the central five volumes and least frequent in
the first and last volumes. Readers of Proust will remember that Balbec
appears very little in the first volume, and the reference to it at the beginning
of "Noms de pays: le nom" is at least somewhat mysterious on the first
reading. Balbec is mentioned chiefly in relation to Legrandin and the

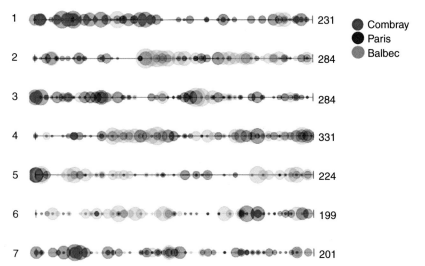

Figure 16 Distribution of references to three settings across the seven volumes of Proust's *In Search of Lost Time*

narrator's grandmother's visits to the seaside town (I: 177). In the first volume of the novel, many of the comparisons between Combray and Paris come through the narrator's engagement with M. de Swann, the father and the son, and his association of that name with Paris, high society, and everything that is not Combray. Balbec all but disappears in the last third of the last volume. The distribution of mentions of places in Proust is correlated with the setting, but mentions of all three places are scattered throughout the volumes. In summary, comparing the distribution of the three primary settings through the seven volumes of the novel in Figure 16, we see the persistence of all three settings throughout the volumes, but we also note that references to Combray dominate the first volume, those to Paris the last volume, and those to Balbec the central volumes.

When we look at textual references to non-French nationalities and places in Proust, we see that the last volume contains the most references to places and people outside of France. Words associated with nationalities and nations similarly follow a consistent pattern we have already seen in Balzac. Figure 17 shows the distribution across the seven volumes of the most common of such words. Words associated with Germans and Germany – that is, variants on "alleman*" like "Allemagne" (Germany) and "allemande" (German) – are the most frequent. Variants on "anglais*" like "anglaise" are the second most common.

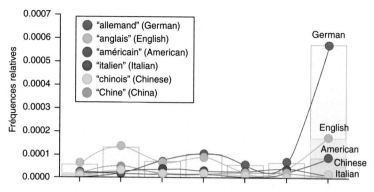

Figure 17 Distribution of sample signifiers of nationality in the seven volumes of Proust's *In Search of Lost Time*

Both of these groups of terms appear most frequently in the final volume of the series, *Time Regained*, which is set partially during World War I and therefore contains many more references to European countries, as well as to places and people outside of France, than the earlier volumes. As a control, we can see that words associated with China ("la Chine") and Chinese ("chinois") are flat across the seven volumes and do not rise in the last volume. The lack of references to China in the last volume is not surprising since most references to China in *In Search of Lost Time* are cultural analogies and not depictions of concrete places, but it does prove that Proust's literary geography is, like Balzac's, built upon a distinction between a peaceful France and a Europe primarily associated with war. This insight is less interesting for Proust scholars, who are well aware of the weight of World War I and national references in *Time Regained*, than for Balzac scholars, for whom war is a less central theme. The persistence of a Balzacian geographical structure in Proust's novels is, however, an unanticipated finding that has been unexplored due to the focus on the primary settings of Paris, Combray, and Balbec. In fact, just as in Balzac, foreign places in Proust are the most likely to be historical, places in Paris are primarily historical, and places in the French provinces are the most likely to be fictional.[12] That said, even many places said to be located near Combray or Balbec that are referred to by invented names exist more or less in the exact geographic location as known historical places.

Even when Proust's characters travel to foreign locations, the relational logic between France and the foreign largely overpowers any exoticism. In the section

---

[12] Furthermore, Proust's archetypical approach (focusing on the "typical" aspects of the city, the village, and the countryside) echoes parts of Balzac's quasi-encyclopedic geographic project, but with far fewer examples of each "type" of place.

"Un Séjour à Venise" of *The Fugitive*, the narrator describes his trip with his mother to the city of Venice, with all of its sensory delights. He uses constant comparisons to Combray and its denizens to understand the novel sensory and cultural ideas presented to him as a young man. One additional complication is that this sequence is remembered in the context of the adult narrator attending a dinner party. The introductory paragraphs focus, however, on the experience of the boy, related in the imperfect tense, suggesting a vague memory that is not fixed at a specific point in the past for him. His experience is thus twice removed from direct experience, being passed through the lens of his earlier life at Combray and remembered at a much later date. This sort of comparison across time is a consistent feature of *In Search of Lost Time*, and one of the reasons place references are less correlated with setting in this volume than they might otherwise be. Indeed, there are almost as many references to Combray in this reminiscence of Venice as there are to the floating city itself.

Looking at the connection between characters and places in *In Search of Lost Time*, we can see that the narrator is associated with by far the most places; indeed, more than two hundred (Table 11). Venice is the foreign place most referenced (21 times) in relation to the narrator.

The characters of *In Search of Lost Time* are also associated with places more or less likely to be historical. Of the characters associated with many places, Charles Swann, the narrator's mother's *mondain* friend, has the most associated historical place references. Much like the cosmopolitan characters we saw in Balzac, Swann connects the narrator's French and Italian world to Germany, the Americas, Asia, and the Pacific; these distant places (in Saint-Thomas, Java, the United Kingdom, the United States) are more likely to use historical toponyms than places in Normandy or the Loire. Françoise, the narrator's housekeeper, has the lowest proportion of historical places associated with her (21%). These places include Parisian locales like the Champs-Elysées. Places with fictional toponyms associated with Françoise include Combray, Guermantes, and other familiar locations central to the narrative. Saint-Loup has a similarly low proportion of references to historical toponyms (31%), due to his association with Doncières, Rivebelle, and the Guermantes family home. Place references associated with other characters like Albertine and Mme Verdurin are split more evenly between fictional and historical places. Both have large numbers of associations to both French and foreign places.

Unlike what we saw with Balzac, place references in Proust do not follow the same gendered or generational patterns where older male characters like military officers and merchants are associated with larger numbers of foreign places. Instead, what we see is that the characters who are central in the novel are associated with more places. The characters associated with the most

Table 11 Characters associated with the most places in Proust's *In Search of Lost Time*

Character	Place references	Percent historical	Distinct associated places	Top associated places
The narrator / Marcel	207	59% (122/207)	56	Venice (21), Balbec (15), Monjouvain (11), Méséglise-La-Vineuese (9), Paris (9), Combray (7)
Albertine	99	54% (54/99)	37	Balbec (8), Montjouvain (8), Incarville (5), Touraine (5), Amsterdam (4), Buttes-Chaumont (4), Paris (4), Trocadéro (4)
Charles Swann	37	73% (27/37)	18	Germany (2), United States, Great Britain, Java, Portugal, Saint-Thomas
Saint-Loup or the Saint-Loups*	26	31% (8/26)	9	Doncières (12), Morocco (5), Rivebelle (2), Touraine (2), Guermantes, Martinville-Le-Sec, Tangier, etc
Mme Verdurin or the Verdurins	25	48% (12/25)	13	La Raspelère (10), Bois de Boulogne (3), Trocadéro (2), Beauvais, Rivebelle, Venice, Pierrefonds, London, etc
Françoise	21	21% (4/21)	15	Combray (5), Roussainville-Le-Pin (3), Saint-André-des-Champs (3), Champs-Elysées (2), Guermantes (2)
Le Baron Charlus	20	55% (11/20)	11	Bois-de-Boulogne (2), Brabant (2), Doncières (2), Saint-Martin-du-Chêne (2), Saint-Pierre-des-Ifs (2)

* not Mme Saint-Loup alone

foreign places in Proust are roughly split between female and male characters; they can be much older than the narrator, like Charlus, or younger like Albertine, or of the same generation like Saint-Loup. Lower-class characters and upper-class characters alike have foreign associations; all characters have more French connections than foreign ones. Aside from Charles Swann, who has far-reaching connections, most characters have a small number of foreign locations associated with them. The lack of association between foreignness and specific social statuses in Proust shows how pervasive foreign references are and how detached place references are from settings.

Another tool we can use to explore connections between characters and places is the network graph. Network graphs that combine characters and places in *In Search of Lost Time* tend to reveal the centrality of the narrator, since he is associated with by far the most places. Figure 18 shows the relations between places outside of France and characters or historical figures.

We can see in Figure 18 that most of the foreign places mentioned in *In Search of Lost Time* are within three or four hops of the narrator and thus connected to the main element of the network graph. Amsterdam, Holland, Morocco, Italy, and many cities in Italy (i.e., Venice, Padua, Trieste, Parma, Pisa, etc.) are all associated directly with the narrator; the two exceptions to this association of places in Italy with the narrator are Milan and Sicily. This Italian world of the narrator marries art, *mondain* society, and literature in a way that reflects his broader interests and social networks in miniature. Many of the characters associated with these places are Italian artists like Giotto, Titian, and Carpaccio, or French writers like Alfred de Musset or Stendhal, who were known to have traveled to or lived in Italy. Others are aristocratic characters like the Prince d'Agrigente and the Princesse de Parme, or influential acquaintances of the narrator like the artist Elstir and the socialite Mme Verdurin. At a distance of two hops, we find Susa, Persia, associated with Mme Dieulafoy, a collector and restorer of Persian artworks, and with Darius and other kings of Persia. Also at two hops, we find Dresden and Twickenham, both associated with Swann and his consort, Odette. Odette is connected to another set of places: Baden-Baden, Bayreuth, Egypt, and Monte Carlo. These far-off places link to Spain, Sicily, Brabant, and Berlin. We can see that these places associated with Odette or Swann are geographically and culturally distinct from the cities of northern Italy that connect to the narrator more directly. Some places and characters are more isolated, such as Florida,

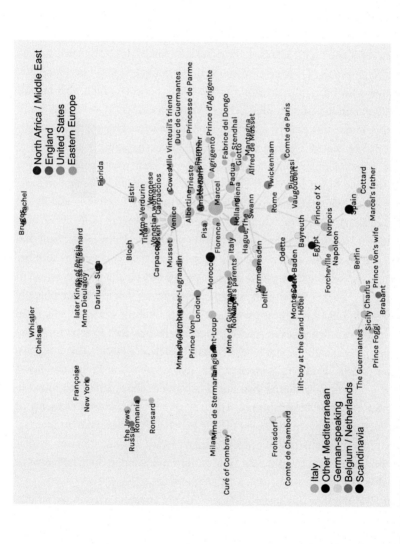

Figure 18 Network graph of characters and places outside of France in Proust's *In Search of Lost Time*

connected only through Elstir but nevertheless part of the main network component.

The most culturally distant places (e.g., New York, Russia, Chelsea) are not connected to the narrator via character associations and, therefore, not integrated into the main network component. Bruges and Frohsdorf are similarly isolated in network terms despite being geographically closer to the world of the narrator. Some places are only connected to one character who has no other significant foreign associations. Rachel is only associated with Bruges in Belgium, Whistler with Chelsea, Françoise is linked to New York but no other foreign places. Of course, many of these characters are, like Françoise, associated with other places within France. The network graph also reveals smaller communities, for example, the subnetworks around Odette and Saint-Loup. One interesting pattern is that cities of the same country are not necessarily closely connected. Chelsea and Twickenham are not closely connected to London. The "German" branch of the network is somewhat more linked but equally close to Egypt and Monte Carlo. Odette is associated with many of these German cities, where she has lived a social life (Baden-Baden) or would like to visit (Bayreuth). We see the same with Bruges, which Rachel visits every year, and Brabant, where the Guermantes family were once Ducs de Brabant and where Charlus claims such a title still; these places lack connections to other characters and serve to define that character space outside the primary world of the narrator. The lack of network association of places that are geographically and culturally linked is a measure of the cosmopolitanism of Proust's fictional world in general, where even working-class characters with French roots can have foreign associations that would be rare in Balzac's world. There are also far more female characters associated with foreign places in Proust and fewer obvious generational patterns than the father-grandfather pattern we found in Balzac for the most far-off places. The patriarchal and imperial elements of Balzac's character hierarchy appear to be lessened in Proust and the commercial aspects of foreign associations are less evident. Many Proustian foreign associations are tied to travel, leisure, or family connections, rather than capitalist or imperial exploits.

Proust's geography has several features that are apparent even in the strictly quantitative elements, such as how many times a place is mentioned. First of all, many fewer distinct places are referenced in Proust, especially in Paris; a related measure is that the average number of times a place is referenced in Proust's Paris is much higher than in Balzac's. We might say that Proust's narrator ruminates over places as opposed to referencing them. Second, the way characters relate to places is less systematic in Proust compared to Balzac; the characters' traits like age, gender, nationality, social class, and profession do not show the same strong patterns as in Balzac, where travel is commonplace for higher-class older men like wealthy merchants and generals. Another way of saying this is that Proust's geography is more freely associated with his character system, which makes sociocultural generalizations more difficult. Third, far more toponyms in Proust are invented than in Balzac; this is especially true in provincial France, less so internationally. Finally, the textual order of place references in Proust is far less tied to setting; where toponyms appear in the text (see Figure 8 versus Figure 16) corresponds less to where the character is located in the story; even in a distant reading of the text, the place-names appear interspersed or jumbled.

This is all to say that Proust's geography is not a conventional realist geography "misremembered" or related through a modernist literary style. The geography is itself impressionistic, discontinuous, hard to localize, and repetitive (Gay, 1999), where Balzac's geography is expansive, frenetic, and rarely returns to any but the most significant places. On the local level, Proust's geographical markers like his train stops and his descriptions of places like landscapes or buildings are more impressionistic, potentially drawing on techniques of the impressionist and post-impressionist school of painters and their theories of visual perception (Gardner, 2019). These two styles (realist and impressionistic) appear also in the presentation of spatial and visual information in the text, in the place references themselves and their diegetic order, as well as in the composition of visual descriptions. The two train lines Proust describes – the little local railway that can be geolocated within an approximate region but whose stops cannot be accurately localized (Figure 14), and the 13h22 train whose stops are given a sequential order that yields an implausible train route (Figure 15) – provide a good example of how impressionist spatial relations mark the text. The impressionism of Proust's geography exists at the level of the place reference, as well as in the style and presentation of particular descriptions. In other words, Proust's underlying literary geography is impressionistic, even without considering his narrative style.

4 Conclusion: Realist versus Post-realist Literary Geographies

Balzac and Proust, as we have seen, follow similar strategies for constructing a literary geography that extends from a local to a global scale. This similarity is evidence that the realist system does not entirely break down between Balzac and Proust. Both great novelistic systems make extensive reference to particular places in Paris, less specific places outside of Paris, fictional places in the French provinces, and abstract or clichéd places outside of France; the broad picture of how place references are assembled fits the pattern of increasing abstraction farther from Paris. Despite this abstraction, a few precise points are included even in the most far-off regions, perhaps more for the narrative effect of realism than for the informational value of those geographical references. Indeed, many references to the Middle East, Asia, the Americas, Africa, and other non-European locations reinforce clichés more than confront them. Rather than an entirely new system, what we find in Proust in comparison to Balzac is an explicit distancing of the fictional world from the historical world. Imaginary places like Combray and Balbec can be placed within a regional and cultural sphere roughly aligned with that of the other places in the story, but they are not historical places, nor does Proust imply they are. By invoking imaginary place-names, rather than fictionalized versions of towns with real names, authors like Proust place a bracket around these experiences and suggest they are somehow outside of history, despite the very concrete references to real towns and cities, events in World War I, and to well-known places in Paris like the Champs-Elysées. In Proust, as in Balzac, this bracketing of the fictional world is mostly localized in the French provinces, which exist largely outside of a traditional historical framework.

While the proportion of place references to regions is similar in Proust's and Balzac's geographies, there are deep rhetorical and psychological differences in how these places are represented. These rhetorical and representational differences matter. Proust's geography cannot be understood without an awareness of the retrospective and rhetorical structure of his novel's narration. Similarly, Balzac's geography cannot be well understood without an intuition of its vastness. For example, if a reader focuses on references to only one *hôtel particulier* without bearing in mind that Balzac references many more, the uniqueness of that place may be overstated. Similarly, if the reader is unaware of reoccurrences of the *hôtel de Guermantes* in Proust's text, one reference might appear overly deterministic of the meaning of that place in one sequence. We cannot entirely dispense with the quantitative approach to literary geography that weights references against the total number of references in that text. Nor can we ignore differences in narrative structure, how place references are integrated into the text rhetorically, or the association of specific characters with places.

I have avoided becoming too embroiled in clichés about realism versus modernism in this Element because I prefer to focus on the nuts and bolts of processing and interpreting place references in the novel. Nevertheless, many of the characteristics of Balzac's geography, including his apparent respect for geographical distances and historical place-names, even when errors or gaps arise, are consistently realist. Proust's geography could be seen as typical of post-realist fiction, whether that fiction is modernist, avant-garde, or pustmodernist. As we have seen in Proust, post-realist or non-realist geography is more relational and less tied to historical frameworks than realist geography. The relation between the character system and geography is also less systematic and predictable the further the novel moves from historical norms. Whereas Balzac aspires to comprehensiveness and inclusion in a way that makes many of his foreign references superficial and clichéd, Proust's geography is partial and his method ruminating, allowing for a deeper engagement of foreign and rarely mentioned places with the narrator's symbolic system. In this sense, Proust and Balzac represent two poles of literary geography: the encyclopedic and the poetic. Other literary geographies can be more like Proust or more like Balzac; they can be more or less comprehensive. The global nature of these literary geographies is always partial, and comprehensiveness is not necessarily an attempt at scientific thoroughness. Indeed, literary geographies can be more encyclopedic than Balzac's without being purely positivistic. For example, Jules Verne's pedagogical geographical fiction is so comprehensive it can be used to teach geography (Donaldson and Kuhlke, 2009), but Verne did not buy into the progressive narrative of science as continuous improvement and worried about the excesses of scientific reason despite his knowledge of scientific advances and technologies (Unwin, 2005). For that reason, despite Balzac's pretentions to scientific objectivity, I am skeptical of attempts to attribute positivist ideology to practitioners of realist literary geography without evidence beyond their referencing of precise historical places.

What have we discovered from our study of literary geographies in French realist and post-realist novels that may be applicable to other fictional worlds? Explicit mentions of place-names like "England" do a very poor job reflecting how important specific places are to a novel, since most references are implicit or layered. For example, counting only the occurrence of the word "Spain" in a text risks missing references to cities, regions, and buildings located in or associated with Spain. Applying an ontology to place references to organize them into hierarchical categories before calculating the weight of those terms makes analytics more meaningful than a simple "bag of words" approach. Geographical maps perform a similar function to ontologies by grouping places together visually so viewers can see where places are densely grouped or sparse. But we must not take these maps as the one true expression of the writer's literary geography. Place references in realist fictions often function as a kind of "effet de réel," in Barthes's term, as when we are told a character grew up in Touraine or traveled to Ghent or Bali (Barthes, 1968), and may play a small role in the fictional world. Some of these places may be primary settings or important associations, but as often, the place references in realist and post-realist fiction give characters depth by endowing them with a past that appears solid and grounded through mentioning places that play minor roles in the fictional world.

The choice of tools to represent literary geography is, therefore, paramount, and maps are not the only option. We must be attentive of how we classify and organize data and of which tools are the most appropriate to the form of literary cartography we are engaged in. Maps work well for distant references that seek to ground the character in a larger fictional world, rather than building a network of associations among places or between places and characters. Close-in references, those references to the places inhabited and experienced by the characters, can be harder to map geographically and may be more fruitfully mapped in their connections with other places or with characters via network graphs or other relational visualizations.

The field of digital literary studies has made great strides in gathering and presenting geographical data (Luchetta, 2017). The next step may be to find ways of presenting relational geographic data in a manner that makes intuitive sense for post-cartographical fiction. The non-Cartesian relationality of places in post-realist geographies means visualizations like network graphs, bubble-lines, and timelines may have more interpretive power for such fictions than conventional maps. When a fictional world shares little to no correspondence with the geography of the globe, techniques such as network analysis can show the connections between characters and places; visualizations like bubblelines or other timelines can reveal how the place references fit together within the text or within the chronology of the plot or narration. These alternative kinds of maps can provide new ways of thinking about literary geography untethered from the model of the globe and the global.

References

Alexander, N. (2015). On Literary Geography. *Literary Geographies*, 1(1), 3–6.

Baker, G. (2009). *Realism's Empire: Empiricism and Enchantment in the Nineteenth-Century Novel*. Columbus: The Ohio State University Press.

Balzac, H. (1855). *La Comédie humaine*, edited by A. Houssiaux, vols. I–XX. Paris: Houssiaux.

Barthes, R. (1968). L'effet de reel, *Communications* (11). Recherches sémiologiques le vraisemblable, 84–89.

Belenky, M. (2020). *Engine of Modernity: The Omnibus and Urban Culture in Nineteenth-Century Paris*. Manchester: Manchester University Press.

Bell, D. (2011). Balzac's Algeria: Realism and the Colonial. *Nineteenth-Century French Studies*, 40(1/2), 35–56.

Bell, D. F. (2010). *Real Time: Accelerating Narrative from Balzac to Zola*. Champaign: University of Illinois Press.

Bender, J., and Marrinan, M. (2010). *The Culture of Diagram*. Stanford, CA: Stanford University Press.

Biggs, M. (1999). Putting the State on the Map: Cartography, Territory, and European State Formation. *Comparative Studies in Society and History*, 44 (2), 374–405.

Bray, P. M. (2013). *The Novel Map: Space and Subjectivity in Nineteenth-Century French Fiction*. Boston: Northeastern University Press.

Brousseau, M. (1996). *Des romans-géographes*. Paris: L'Harmattan.

Brousseau, M., and Cambron, M. (2003). Entre géographie et littérature: frontières et perspectives dialogiques. *Recherches sociographiques*, 44(3), 525–547.

Brunetière, F. (1906). *Honoré de Balzac, 1799–1850*. Paris: Calmann-Lévy.

Bui, V., and Le Huenen, R. (eds.). (2017). *Balzac et la Chine: la Chine et Balzac*. Rouen: Presses universitaires de Rouen et du Havre.

Bushell, S. (2016). Mapping Fiction: Spatialising the Literary Work. *Literary Mapping in the Digital Age*. London: Routledge, 143–164.

Cerfberr, A., and Christophe, J.-F. (1902). *Repertory of the* Comédie humaine. Philadelphia, PA: Avil.

Chambers, R. (1969). *Gérard de Nerval et la poétique de l'espace*. Paris: José Corti.

Cnockaert, V. (2009). L'Empire de l'ensauvagement: adieu de Balzac. *Romantisme* (145), 37–49.

Collot, M. (2014). *Pour une géographie littéraire*. Paris: José Corti.

Conley, T. (1996). *The Self-Made Map: Cartographic Writing in Early Modern France*. Minneapolis: University of Minnesota Press.

Conroy, M. (2021). Networks, Maps, and Time: Visualizing Historical Networks using Palladio. *DHQ: Digital Humanities Quarterly*, 15 (1).

Cooper, D., Donaldson, C., and Murrieta-Flores, P. (eds.) (2016). *Literary Mapping in the Digital Age*. Abingdon: Routledge.

Dear, M., Ketchum, J., Luria, S., and Richardson, D. (2011). *GeoHumanities: Art, History, Text at the Edge of Place*. Abingdon: Routledge.

Donaldson, D. P., and Kuhlke, O. (2009). Jules Verne's *Around the World in Eighty Days*: Helping Teach the National Geography Standards. *Journal of Geography*, 108(2), 39–46.

Dufour, P., Mozet, N., and Andréoli, M. (2004). *Balzac géographe: territoires*. Saint-Cyr-sur-Loire, France: C. Pirot.

Dupuy, L. (2019). *L'Imaginaire géographique: essai de géographie littéraire*. Pau: Presses de l'Université de Pau et des Pays de l'Adour.

Ferré, A. (1939). *Géographie de Marcel Proust*. Sablons, France: Sagittaire.

Gardner, D. (2019). Landscapes and Perceptual Distortions in Proust. *Nineteenth-Century French Studies*, *48*(1), 130–148.

Gay, J. C. (1999). L'Espace discontinu de Marcel Proust. *Expressions* (13), 15–33.

Genette, G. (1983). *Narrative Discourse: An Essay in Method*. Ithaca, NY: Cornell University Press.

Guichardet, J. (1986). *Balzac, "archéologue" de Paris*. Paris: Slatkine.

Heuser, R., Algee-Hewitt, M., and Lockhart, A. (2016). Mapping the Emotions of London in Fiction, 1700–1900: A Crowdsourcing Experiment. *Literary Mapping in the Digital Age*. London: Routledge, 43–64.

Hill, L. L. (2009). *Georeferencing: The Geographic Associations of Information*. Cambridge, MA: MIT Press.

Hoffman, L. -F. (1965). *Répertoire géographique de* La Comédie humaine *de Balzac*, vol. I, *L'Étranger*. Paris: José Corti.

Hoffman, L.-F. (1968). *Répertoire géographique de* La Comédie humaine *de Balzac*, vol. II, *La Province*. Paris: José Corti.

Hones, S. (2008). Text As It Happens: Literary Geography. *Geography Compass*, 2(5),1301–1317.

Kristeva, J. (1994). *Le Temps sensible: Proust et l'expérience littéraire*. Paris: Gallimard.

Landy, J. (2004). *Philosophy As Fiction: Self, Deception, and Knowledge in Proust*. Oxford: Oxford University Press.

Lionnet, F. (1993). Créolité in the Indian Ocean: Two Models of Cultural Diversity. *Yale French Studies*, 101–112.

Lionnet, F. (1992). "Logiques métisses": Cultural Appropriation and Postcolonial Representations. *College Literature*, 19(3/1), 100–120.

Luchetta, S. (2017). Exploring the Literary Map: An Analytical Review of Online Literary Mapping Projects. *Geography Compass*, 11(1), e12303.

McDonald, C., and Suleiman, S. (eds.). (2010) *French Global: A New Approach to Literary History*. New York: Columbia University Press.

Moncla, L., Gaio, M., Joliveau, T., and Lay, Y. F. L. (2017). Automated Geoparsing of Paris Street Names in 19th Century Novels. *Proceedings of the 1st ACM SIGSPATIAL Workshop on Geospatial Humanities*. Association for Computing Machinery: New York 1–8.

Moretti, F. (1999). *Atlas of the European Novel, 1800–1900*. London: Verso.

Piatti, B. (2008). *Die Geographie der Literatur. Schauplätze, Handlungsräume, Raumphantasien*. Göttingen: Wallstein.

Piatti, B., Bär, H.R., Reuschel, A.K., Hurni, L., and Cartwright, W. (2009). Mapping Literature: Towards a Geography of Fiction. *Cartography and Art*, Springer: Berlin, Heidelberg, 1–16.

Prasad, P. (2003). Espace colonial et vérité historique dans *Indiana*. *Études littéraires*, 35 (2–3), 71–85.

Prendergast, C. (1986). *The Order of Mimesis: Balzac, Stendhal, Nerval, Flaubert*. Cambridge: Cambridge University Press.

Proust, M. (1946). *À la recherche du temps perdu*, 7 vols. Paris: Gallimard.

Pugh, A. (1974). *Balzac's Recurring Characters*. Toronto: University of Toronto Press.

Raser, G. B. (1964). *Guide to Balzac's Paris*. Choisy-Le-Roi: Imprimerie de France.

Raser, G. B. (1970). *The Heart of Balzac's Paris*. Choisy-Le-Roi: Imprimerie de France.

Risam, R., and Josephs, K. B. (eds.). (2021). *The Digital Black Atlantic*. Minneapolis: University of Minnesota Press.

Robb, G. (1995). *Balzac: A Biography*, London: W. W. Norton and Company.

Robb, G. (2008). *The Discovery of France*, London: W. W. Norton and Company.

Schivelbusch, W. (1986). *The Railway Journey: The Industrialization of Time and Space in the 19th Century*, Berkeley: University of California Press.

Solina, F., and Ravnik, R. (2010). Georeferencing Works of Literature. *Proceedings of the ITI 2010, 32nd International Conference on Information Technology Interfaces*, 249–254.

Unwin, T. (2005). Jules Verne: Negotiating Change in the Nineteenth Century. *Science Fiction Studies*, 32:1, 5–17.

Westphal, B. (2011). *La géocritique: réel, fiction, espace*. Paris: Minuit.

Related Online Projects

Atlas of Fiction. www.atlasoffiction.com

CNRS / Université Sorbonne nouvelle – Paris 3 / ENS. Vers une géographie littéraire. Programme de recherche de l'UMR 7172 THALIM (Théorie et histoire des arts et des littératures de la modernité) Équipe "Écritures de la modernité. geographielitteraire.hypotheses.org/a-propos

Spatial Humanities: Texts, GIS and Places. www.lancaster.ac.uk/spatialhum/index.html/

Piatti, Barbara, et al. (2006). *Ein literarischer Atlas Europas* www.literaturatlas.eu

Sources and Methods

Data

The place references for this project came from four main sources.

Ferré, A. (1939). *Géographie de Marcel Proust*, Sagittaire: Sablons, France. (Mapping Proust).

Hoffman, L.-F. (1965). *Répertoire géographique de La Comédie humaine de Balzac, vol. I, L'Étranger*. Paris: José Corti (Mapping Balzac – World).

Hoffman, L.-F. (1968). *Répertoire géographique de La Comédie humaine de Balzac, vol. II, La Province*. Paris: José Corti (Mapping Balzac – The Provinces).

Raser, G. B. (1964). *Guide to Balzac's Paris*. Choisy-Le-Roi: Imprimerie de France (Mapping Balzac – Paris).

The data from these repertories were scanned and converted to text whereupon I spent a good amount of time cleaning and recategorizing data and correcting issues with the geographical hierarchies and ontology or with the underlying structure of the data. For example, I removed references to countries that no longer exist, added missing regions for places that had not been classified, and deleted duplicates. Next, I geocoded the data, first automatically and then by hand for those places that could not be automatically matched. Geocoding the Paris data was the most laborious, as the majority of places needed to be manually geocoded and many of the places required a good amount of detective work to locate, including using atlases and dictionaries of historical Paris held in the Stanford Libraries and the David Rumsey Map Collections. The geographical data are now available online as raw data in tab-separated value files (tsv) and as formatted javascript (json) files for anyone who would like to work directly with the data or contribute corrections on either GitHub (www.github.com/mrconroy/mapping-balzac) or Figshare (www.doi.org/10.6084/m9.figshare.14925177.v1).

Texts

In order to digitally process place references and to calculate word counts, I have used the following editions of both Proust and Balzac:

Balzac, H. (1855). *La Comédie humaine*, edited by A. Houssiaux, vols I–IV, Paris: Houssiaux.

Proust, M. (1946). *À la recherche du temps perdu* (7 volumes). Paris: Gallimard.

To generate the counts of place references, I primarily used Open Refine, a data-processing suite that works with multivariate or messy data and is ideal for use in the humanities for that reason. This suite makes easy applying multiple filters at the same time or using scripts to make calculations; other tools that can perform the same functions are Excel pivot tables or in R.

Visualizations

To create maps and network diagrams, I primarily used Palladio, a tool for visualizing historical and humanities data available via web browser or for download via GitHub: https://hdlab.stanford.edu/palladio/. The javascript files I have made available are preformatted to work in Palladio. Palladio allows the user to filter data sets and change map settings such as the basemap, colors, and other design features; it is also possible to make network graphs and networked maps with Palladio (Conroy, 2021). To create the graphs of word occurrences and bubbleline visualizations, I used Voyant Tools: www.voyant-tools.org. Finally, interactive versions of all map visualizations in this Element are available via Tableau Public. These maps can be filtered by book or series so researchers can produce maps for individual books without having to work from the raw data: https:public.tableau.com/profile/melanie.conroy/

Figures

Figures 1, 2, 5, 6, and 14 were produced by the author in Palladio using the "map" feature. Figures 10 and 18 were produced in Palladio using the "graph" feature and recolored in Adobe Photoshop by the author.

Figure 3 appears courtesy of the Bibliothèque Nationale de France and was downloaded from its online library (www.gallica.bnf.fr) in December 2020.

Figures 4 and 7 appear courtesy of the David Rumsey Map Collection and were downloaded from their website (www.davidrumsey.com) in December 2020.

Figures 13 and 15 were created in Adobe Photoshop by the author, based on André Ferré's maps in his *Géographie de Marcel Proust* (1939).

Figures 8, 9, 16, and 17 were created by the author using the Voyant Tools website (www.voyant-tools.org/) in January 2020.

Acknowledgments

I would like to thank the editors of the Digital Literary Studies series, the anonymous reviewers of this Element, and the office staff at Cambridge University Press who worked through the pandemic to bring this project to fruition. Earlier research for this Element was completed with support from the University of Memphis College of Arts and Sciences, including funding for my research assistant Jessica Collins, who corrected the data on Balzac's characters and their associations with specific places. For the writing of the manuscript, I benefited from a Deborah Talbot Research grant. For their support over the years, I would like to thank my family and my colleagues Joshua Landy, Hans Ulrich Gumbrecht, Laura Wittman, Dan Edelstein, Maria Comsa, Chloe Edmondson, Nicole Coleman, Chad Pedrioli, Elizabeth Coggeshall, Darci Gardner, and the many others who discussed this project with me or who read early drafts. I presented early versions of the ideas and visualizations in this Element at the Nineteenth-Century French Studies conference and the American Comparative Literature Association, where I received valuable feedback from participants.

Cambridge Elements ☰

Digital Literary Studies

Katherine Bode
Australian National University

Katherine Bode is Professor of Literary and Textual Studies at the Australian National University. Her research explores the critical potential and limitations of computational approaches to literature, in publications including *A World of Fiction: Digital Collections and the Future of Literary History* (2018), *Advancing Digital Humanities: Research, Methods, Theories* (2014), *Reading by Numbers: Recalibrating the Literary Field* (2012) and *Resourceful Reading: The New Empiricism, eResearch and Australian Literary Culture* (2009).

Adam Hammond
University of Toronto

Adam Hammond is Assistant Professor of English at the University of Toronto. He is author of *Literature in the Digital Age* (Cambridge 2016) and co-author of *Modernism: Keywords* (2014). He works on modernism, digital narrative, and computational approaches to literary style. He is editor of the forthcoming *Cambridge Companion to Literature in the Digital Age* and *Cambridge Critical Concepts: Literature and Technology*.

Gabriel Hankins
Clemson University

Gabriel Hankins is Associate Professor of English at Clemson University. His first book is *Interwar Modernism and the Liberal World Order* (Cambridge 2019). He writes on modernism, digital humanities, and color. He is technical manager for the Twentieth Century Literary Letters Project and co-editor on *The Digital Futures of Graduate Study in the Humanities* (in progress).

Advisory Board

About the Series
Our series provides short exemplary texts that address a pressing research question of clear scholarly interest within a defined area of literary studies, clearly articulate the method used to address the question, and demonstrate the literary insights achieved.

Cambridge Elements☰

Digital Literary Studies

Elements in the Series

Can We Be wrong? The Problem of Textual Evidence in a Time of Data
Andrew Piper

Literary Geographies in Balzac and Proust
Melanie Conroy

A full series listing is available at: www.cambridge.org/EDLS

Printed in the United States
by Baker & Taylor Publisher Services